DEVELOPING QUESTIONING TECHNIQUES

A Self-concept Approach

ARTHUR A. CARIN

Queens College

ROBERT B. SUND

University of Northern Colorado

CHARLES E. MERRILL PUBLISHING COMPANY

A Bell & Howell Company *Columbus, Ohio*

International Standard Book Number: *0–675–09184–5*

Library of Congress Catalog Card Number: *77–173876*

6 7 8 9 10 / 81 80 79 78 77

Printed in the United States of America

PREFACE

When asked the characteristics of an outstanding teacher, people often rank as primary a teacher's ability to interrelate with students in personal humane ways. Paramount in doing this is the ability to question, accept responses, and sincerely and wisely listen to students. This book presents practical suggestions for teachers in selecting and using appropriate questioning techniques. The stress throughout is upon using questions not only for assisting student cognitive achievement and level of understanding, but as an aid in the building of student self-esteem and creativity.

Learning to elicit superior and more diverse responses from students will enable the teacher to stress higher cognitive levels of thinking, give more attention to the affective areas of instruction, and teach for the multi-talents of students rather than to stress only academic ability.

One chapter emphasizes the student's impression of "self" in order to build self-esteem. In an era of growing humanistic concern for the individual, the questioning procedures here presented are vital for teachers to explore. Another chapter is concerned with developing creative thinking, encouraging critical analysis, and actively involving the learner in teaching-learning for his personal development. The works of Benjamin Bloom and Jerome Bruner are presented along with practical suggestions for *active* involvement of the learner.

Chapters delve into specific questioning techniques using Benjamin Bloom's Cognitive and Affective Domains. Guidelines are provided for writing and using questions for these two important aspects of learning. Ways of using questions to stimulate creativity in all curricular areas such as discussions, evaluations, audio-visual aides, etc. are given, and format guides are provided for writing and using questions of this type. Specific techniques in applying text materials to films, filmstrips, slides, film loops, tapes, bulletin boards, and invitations to discover are provided. The final chapter deals with procedures to help teachers evaluate and modify their questioning techniques to insure improvement. Methods for evaluating questioning skills include checking for convergency and divergency, classifying questions according to Bloom's Taxonomy, for critical thinking processes, student-teacher interaction analysis, general questioning ability, total time analysis, and discovery teaching analysis.

The techniques outlined in this book have been tried with hundreds of perspective and experienced teachers and gleaned from these teachers in university classrooms and inservice workshops.

Terry, Jill, Amy, and Jon Carin are acknowledged for their long suffering and frequently asked *convergent* question: "Can we go on vacation this time or do you have more writing to do?"

A. A. C.

R. B. S.

CONTENTS

1

HELPING THE "PERSON" BECOME

Many educators believe that education today is moving toward a new era of humanism. For over a century the educational complex has adopted industrial technological techniques to its purposes; students have been regimented, grouped, re-grouped, and involved in national curriculum projects with little regard to their inclinations, interests, motives, or desires. Who has listened to the students, valued their thoughts, feelings, and varied potential talents?

Just as the workers in overly-mechanized industrial plants have been alienated, so have many of our youth. Some of them have resorted to establishing their own music, poetry, dress, hair styles, and modes of conduct, most of which are the antithesis of tradition. Our alienated youth coast through adolescence and beyond seeking new meaning, and vainly experiment with drugs, yogi, oriental mysticism, sensitivity training, etc., in attempts to find their identity. The American dream of a beautiful existence presents mental conflict for them because of its inconsistencies. America is beautiful, but it is polluted. America is beautiful, but her people are intolerant. America is beautiful, but it is packed with ghettos. America is beautiful, but many of its people starve. America is beautiful, but its citizens often become robots for the sake of technology.

To this generation, the "person" becoming a sensitive, loving, total human is central to their dream. Listen to their music, and poetry, and contrast it with that of the older generation to realize what is meant by the generation gap.

By the time of adolescence, many students' views toward life are diverse from their parents, causing great difficulty in communication. Teachers who listen, who are sensitive, aware, and accept with dedication the need to help students become better persons, do much to aid these students to stay alive and pass into society. It is our view that American education is beginning a new renaissance, a rebirth, that stresses and values the manifestation of all a person's talents, not just his academic skills. The tradition-bound teacher believes if students repeat memorized knowledge, they become educated. A modern, affective teacher believes in the importance of building a person's "self-concept" through identifying and developing his talents. We humans are a complex of numerous abilities and skills. Every person is talented in many respects: creative in art or music; adept in organizing, communicating, socializing; drawn toward mechanical, academic, or critical thinking skills, etc. By becoming involved in activities utilizing these talents, the individual builds his "self-concept," giving him feelings of security and contributing to his identity. As educators, we must view a student not as a sponge meant to soak up information, but as an individual in the process of becoming. The task of the contemporary instructor is to facilitate the discovery and growth of all of those entities that make a human a whole person. While this is a tremendous responsibility, it is also a beautiful goal for a teacher.

Involved in any deep communication between persons is the ability to ask appropriate questions and to listen. This is the genius of communication. To listen and question at just the right place and degree delimits the truly brilliant instructor from the average. An insightful question appropriately delivered may stimulate the individual to reach a new level of mental mediation. We learn to think only by thinking. We become creative only by having opportunities to be creative. A properly phrased question often is the necessary "input" needed to ignite the student's thinking and creative processes.

When a teacher asks a question, he is giving a student the opportunity to use his mind. If the instructor asks only questions requiring regurgitation of previously presented information, the student has only opportunities to repeat what he has memorized. However, if a teacher asks a question such as, "How would you solve the problem?" he is giving the student opportunities to use and develop many of his mental capabilities. Clearly, the questions a teacher asks can make the difference between an antiquated educational wasteland and an exciting learning environment.

Teachers identified as outstanding by students are those who related well with them. Students, when asked, "Who were your great teachers?" seldom state first that the teacher was outstanding because he knew his subject matter. They usually say, "He was a great teacher because he was really interested in me. He gave me a lot of help. He was excited when I learned," etc. Subject matter competence is important, but it is secondary to how a teacher interrelates with his students. There are many good, academically "C-average" teachers, and there are too many poor, academically "A-average" teachers. If to teach well were mainly dependent on academic competence, all a superintendent would have to do is hire those teachers with the most subject matter courses and the best grades. There would be no need for an interview and recommendations. A moment's reflection on this clearly indicates that teaching is more than being academically competent.

What does a good teacher do? He gets to know and appreciate his student's needs, aspirations, competencies, and talents. He values them as people and is excited in contributing to their growth. He facilitates learning, prizes, accepts, and trusts students and is empathetically understanding.[1] In private conversations with students, he asks questions to elicit responses about themselves. For example:

Where do you come from?
Where were you born?
What do you like?
What don't you like?
What do you want to learn?
How would you like to learn?
What do you want to become?
What do you think would be the best way for you to become that?
How are things going at home?
What "turns you on"?
What is your favorite song?
What is your favorite story?
If you could do anything you wanted today, what would you do?
How do you feel about that?
What makes you sad?

---

[1] Rogers, Carl, *Humanizing Education*. Washington, D.C.: Association for Supervision and Curriculum Development, NEA, 1967, pp. 1–17.

What makes you happy?
What makes you laugh or cry?
What do you think are your strongest attributes?
What do you do well?
What do you need to improve?
How can I help?
What's great about this course?
What's wrong with this course?
How could I improve as a teacher?
What do we need to do to improve this course, school, etc.

SELF-ESTEEM

Generally, any instructor in upper elementary, junior high, and senior high school should attempt to assess his students self-esteem early in the year. How and what a student thinks he is capable of doing is the best predictor of what he will do when confronted with a task. If a student's self-esteem is poor, he thinks, for example, that he can't do mathematics, the instructor should be aware of this so he can do as much as possible to build the confidence of the student.

There are many self-esteem inventories available through various sources. Shown below is an example of one developed by James K. Hoffmeister. The approach toward assessment exemplified in this questionnaire is congruent with the humanistic or personal emphasis described above. The questionnaire instructions are intended to facilitate communication with the respondent about what information the questions are designed to provide. The questions themselves are intended to be clear, unambiguous, and to provide maximum information about how the student views himself and how he feels about himself in various situations. The rather clear concern of such a measurement strategy is to ensure, as much as possible, that the way one chooses to seek information does not, in itself, conflict with or bring into question the stated goals of trying to provide a more humane, person-oriented learning environment. It is suggested that you use this questionnaire as a guide and try to construct an inventory that will provide information about attitudes of concern to you or your students. (Note, a separate sheet, not included here, is used for marking the responses.) The construction of such an inventory will not only give you some insights into how questionnaires are prepared, but will sensitize you to some of the side effects that may occur as a result of the way tests are developed and used.

SELF-ESTEEM QUESTIONNAIRE[2]

Form SR1

The following items have been selected because we think they may provide an estimate of your feelings of self-esteem. By self-esteem we mean how you feel about yourself. If you have high self-esteem, you would probably feel positively about yourself. That is, you would probably think that the way you perform or get along in most situations is satisfactory and that, in general, other people like and accept you. If, on the other hand, you have low self-esteem, this would probably mean that you thought that you did not get along very well in most situations. You would probably feel that you did not do as good a job as others expected you to do. And you might think that other people felt that you could not do things satisfactorily most of the time, and that they did not really think too highly of you as a person.

There are five possible responses for each question. For example, look at the statement below.

1. I feel sure of myself.

(1) Yes, very much	(3) Depends	(4) Only a little
(2) Quite a bit		(5) No, not at all

If you feel that you generally are very sure of yourself, then you would fill in the space marked with a number 1 opposite number one on your answer sheet. 1. 1 2 3 4 5 If you felt that sometimes you were sure of yourself and other times you were not, in other words it depended upon the situation, then you would fill in the space marked with a number 3. 1. 1 2 3 4 5

There are a number of statements followed by the question, "Does the situation described in number _____ upset you?" These questions always refer back to the previous statement and are included in order to provide more complete information about how you really feel about these situations.

Please do *not* respond to any statement you feel is ambiguous, for we will not know how to interpret your response. If you would care to write any comments about such items or if you would like to add some comments about yourself which would increase our understanding of you, please feel free to do so on the back of your answer sheet.

[2] Copyright, 1971, by James K. Hoffmeister, all rights reserved. Test Analysis and Development Corporation, 855 Inca Parkway, Boulder, Colo. 80303. Information about cost and scoring is available at the above address.

There are no right or wrong answers to these items. Rather, your response simply indicates how you feel about yourself. Remember, your response to any question should indicate how you *usually* feel—not just an occasional type of thing.

1. I feel sure of myself.

   (1) Yes, very much (3) Depends (4) Only somewhat
   (2) Pretty much (5) No, not at all

2. Most of my friends accept me as much as they accept other people.

   (1) Yes, very much so (3) Depends (4) Only somewhat so
   (2) Pretty much so (5) No, not at all so

3. Does the situation described in number 2 upset you?

   (1) Yes, very much (3) Depends (4) Only a little
   (2) Quite a bit (5) No, not at all

4. Most people who are important to me, who know me, think I do most things well.

   (1) Yes, very much (3) I'm not sure (4) Only somewhat
   (2) Pretty much (5) No, not at all

5. Does the situation described in number 4 upset you?

   (1) Yes, very much (3) Depends (4) Only a little
   (2) Quite a bit (5) No, not at all

6. Most persons my own age seem to be able to do things better than I.

   (1) Yes, very much (3) Depends (4) Only a little
   (2) Quite a bit (5) No, not at all

7. Does the situation described in number 6 upset you?

   (1) Yes, very much (3) Depends (4) Only a little
   (2) Quite a bit (5) No, not at all

8. I'm usually a lot of fun to be with.

   (1) Yes, very much so (3) I'm not sure (4) Only somewhat so
   (2) Pretty much so (5) No, not at all so

9. Does the situation described in number 8 upset you?

   (1) Yes, very much (3) Depends (4) Only a little
   (2) Quite a bit (5) No, not at all

10. Most persons who I want to do things with really want me to do things with them.

    (1) Yes, very much so (3) I'm not sure (4) Only somewhat so
    (2) Pretty much so (5) No, not at all so

11. Does the situation described in number 10 upset you?
    (1) Yes, very much (2) Quite a bit (3) Depends (4) Only a little (5) No, not at all

12. I'm satisfied with the way I handle *most* situations.
    (1) Yes, very much (2) Pretty much (3) Depends (4) Only somewhat (5) No, not at all

13. I'm popular with most people.
    (1) Yes, very much (2) Pretty much (3) I'm not sure (4) Only a little (5) No, not at all

14. Does the situation described in number 13 upset you?
    (1) Yes, very much (2) Quite a bit (3) Depends (4) Only a little (5) No, not at all

15. Most people my own age seem to be able to do things easier than I.
    (1) Yes, very much (2) Pretty much (3) Depends (4) Only somewhat (5) No, not at all

16. Does the situation described in number 15 upset you?
    (1) Yes, very much (2) Quite a bit (3) Depends (4) Only a little (5) No, not at all

17. Other people who are important to me really accept me.
    (1) Yes, very much (2) Pretty much (3) I'm not sure (4) Only a little (5) No, not at all

18. Does the situation described in number 17 upset you?
    (1) Yes, very much (2) Quite a bit (3) Depends (4) Only a little (5) No, not at all

19. Most people my own age are more satisfied with themselves than I am with myself.
    (1) Yes, very much (2) Quite a bit (3) Depends (4) Only a little (5) No, not at all

20. Does the situation described in number 19 upset you?
    (1) Yes, very much (2) Quite a bit (3) Depends (4) Only a little (5) No, not at all

21. What would be your best description of your feelings of self-confidence?
    (1) Not at all self-confident (2) Only a little self-confident (3) Depends on the situation (4) Pretty self-confident (5) Very self-confident

SELF-ESTEEM QUESTIONNAIRE[3]

Form TR1

(Staff Rating)

The following items have been selected because we think they may provide an estimate of a person's feelings of self-esteem. By self-esteem we mean how a person feels about himself. If a person has high self-esteem, he would probably feel positively about himself. That is, he would probably think that the way he performs or gets along in most situations is satisfactory and that, in general, other people like and accept him. If, on the other hand, the person has low self-esteem, this would probably mean that he thought that he did not get along very well in most situations. He would probably feel that he did not do as good a job as others expected him to do. And he might think that other people felt that he could not do things satisfactorily most of the time, and that they did not really think too highly of him as a person.

There are five possible responses for each question. For example, look at the statement below.

1. Does he (she) feel positively about himself (herself)?

(1) No, not at all (3) Depends (4) Quite a bit
(2) Only a little (5) Yes, very much

If you feel that the person generally feels positively about himself, then you would circle the number 5 on your answer sheet. If you felt that sometimes the person felt positively about himself and other times he did not, in other words it depended upon the situation, then you would circle the number 3 on your answer sheet.

Please do *not* respond to any statement you feel is ambiguous, for we will not know how to interpret your response. If you would care to write any comments about such items or if you would like to add some comments about the person which would increase our understanding of your responses, please feel free to do so on the back of your answer sheet.

There are no right or wrong responses to these items. Rather, your response simply indicates how you think the person feels about himself. Remember, your response to any question should indicate how you think the person *usually* feels—not just an occasional type of thing. Please *circle* the response number that best describes the person.

If you feel that you do not know the person well enough to be reasonably sure of your response, please do *not* circle any response number for the person on that question.

---

[3] Copyright, 1971, by James K. Hoffmeister, all rights reserved. Test Analysis and Development Corporation, 855 Inca Parkway, Boulder, Colo. 80303. Information about cost and scoring is available at the above address.

1. Does he (she) feel positively about himself (herself)?
   (1) No, not at all (3) Depends (4) Quite a bit
   (2) Only a little (5) Yes, very much

2. Is he (she) usually tense and nervous?
   (1) No, not at all (3) Depends (4) Quite a bit
   (2) Only a little (5) Yes, very much

3. Does he (she) feel sure of himself (herself)?
   (1) No, not at all (3) Depends (4) Quite a bit
   (2) Only a little (5) Yes, very much

4. Do his (her) feelings get hurt easily?
   (1) No, not at all (3) Depends (4) Quite a bit
   (2) Only a little (5) Yes, very much

5. What would be your best estimate of his (her) feelings of self-confidence?
   (1) Not at all self-confident (4) Pretty self-confident
   (2) Only somewhat self-confident (5) Very self-confident
   (3) Depends on the situation

6. Is he (she) popular with most people?
   (1) No, not at all (3) Depends (4) Quite a bit
   (2) Only a little (5) Yes, very much

7. To what extent is he (she) upset by what other people think about him (her)?
   (1) No, not at all (3) Depends (4) Quite a bit
   (2) Only a little (5) Yes, very much

____________________ ____________________

Name of person rated *Rater*

Questionnaires

Note in the preceding questionnaires that there is one for the student and one for the instructor. It is suggesed that a teacher rate how he perceives students prior to the time he obtains the responses from their questionnaires. He should then analyze the two responses and compare his perceptions with theirs. In this way he will increase his perceptual acuity of persons and become more aware and sensitive.

CLASSROOM ATMOSPHERE

A second test, also developed by James K. Hoffmeister, uses a similar approach for the measurement of classroom atmosphere. As before, the purpose of the test is discussed with the respondent in the instruction section of the test, and examples are provided to clarify the intent of the questions.

CLASSROOM ATMOSPHERE QUESTIONNAIRE[4]

Form SR1

The following items have been selected because we think they may provide an estimate of the kind of atmosphere in your classroom. By classroom atmosphere we mean how you feel about the things that have happened to you in your classroom. In some classrooms you may feel like you get the kind of help you need and that you are accepted and treated as a worthwhile person. You probably like to go to such classrooms. In other classrooms you may feel like you are not really accepted or treated as an individual, and that you are given little help in learning the things you do not know. You may feel like you do not even want to go near such classrooms.

There are five possible responses for each question. For example, look at the statement below.

Your Teacher:

1. Respects your ideas and concerns.

(1) Never	(3) Depends	(4) Usually
(2) Seldom		(5) Always

If you feel that your teacher always respects your ideas and concerns, then you would fill in the space marked with a number 5 opposite number one on your answer sheet. 1. 1 2 3 4 5 If you feel that sometimes your teacher respects your ideas and concerns and other times does not, in other words it depends upon the situation, then you would fill in the space marked with a number 3. 1. 1 2 3 4 5

[4] Copyright, 1971, by James K. Hoffmeister, all rights reserved. Test Analysis and Development Corporation, 855 Inca Parkway, Boulder, Colo. 80303. Information about cost and scoring is available at the above address.

There are a number of statements followed by the question, "Does the situation described in number — upset you?" These questions always refer back to the previous statement and are included in order to provide more complete information about how you really feel about these situations.

Please do *not* respond to any statement you feel is ambiguous, for we will not know how to interpret your response. If you would care to write any comments about such items or if you would like to add some comments which would increase our understanding of your feelings about the things that happen to you in your classroom, please feel free to do so on the back of your answer sheet.

There are no right or wrong answers to these items. Rather, your response simply indicates how you feel about the things that have happened to you in your classroom. Remember, your response to any question should indicate how you *usually* feel—not just an occasional type of thing.

Your Teacher:

1. Respects your ideas and concerns.

   (1) Never (3) Depends (4) Usually
   (2) Seldom (5) Always

2. Does the situation described in #1 upset you?

   (1) Yes, very much (3) Depends (4) Only a little
   (2) Quite a bit (5) No, not at all

3. Helps you to develop skills in understanding others.

   (1) Never (3) Depends (4) Usually
   (2) Seldom (5) Always

4. Does the situation described in #3 upset you?

   (1) Yes, very much (3) Depends (4) Only a little
   (2) Quite a bit (5) No, not at all

5. Accepts your feelings.

   (1) Never (3) Depends (4) Usually
   (2) Seldom (5) Always

6. Does the situation described in #5 upset you?

   (1) Yes, very much (3) Depends (4) Only a little
   (2) Quite a bit (5) No, not at all

7. Is enthusiastic about working with you.

   (1) Never (3) Depends (4) Usually
   (2) Seldom (5) Always

8. Does the situation described in #7 upset you?
   (1) Yes, very much (2) Quite a bit (3) Depends (4) Only a little (5) No, not at all
9. Sees you as a responsible person.
   (1) Never (2) Seldom (3) Depends (4) Usually (5) Always
10. Does the situation described in #9 upset you?
   (1) Yes, very much (2) Quite a bit (3) Depends (4) Only a little (5) No, not at all
11. Helps you to develop skills in separating fact from opinion.
   (1) Never (2) Seldom (3) Depends (4) Usually (5) Always
12. Does the situation described in #11 upset you?
   (1) Yes, very much (2) Quite a bit (3) Depends (4) Only a little (5) No, not at all
13. Likes you.
   (1) Never (2) Seldom (3) Depends (4) Usually (5) Always
14. Does the situation described in #13 upset you?
   (1) Yes, very much (2) Quite a bit (3) Depends (4) Only a little (5) No, not at all
15. Helps you to develop skills in understanding yourself.
   (1) Never (2) Seldom (3) Depends (4) Usually (5) Always
16. Does the situation described in #15 upset you?
   (1) Yes, very much (2) Quite a bit (3) Depends (4) Only a little (5) No, not at all
17. Treats you fairly.
   (1) Never (2) Seldom (3) Depends (4) Usually (5) Always
18. Does the situation described in #17 upset you?
   (1) Yes, very much (2) Quite a bit (3) Depends (4) Only a little (5) No, not at all
19. Helps you to develop skills in communicating with others.
   (1) Never (2) Seldom (3) Depends (4) Usually (5) Always

20. Does the situation described in #19 upset you?

(1) Yes, very much (3) Depends (4) Only a little
(2) Quite a bit (5) No, not at all

21. Helps you individually when you need it.

(1) Never (3) Depends (4) Usually
(2) Seldom (5) Always

22. Does the situation described in #21 upset you?

(1) Yes, very much (3) Depends (4) Only a little
(2) Quite a bit (5) No, not at all

23. Helps you to develop skills in listening.

(1) Never (3) Depends (4) Usually
(2) Seldom (5) Always

24. Does the situation described in #23 upset you?

(1) Yes, very much (3) Depends (4) Only a little
(2) Quite a bit (5) No, not at all

25. Is easy to talk to.

(1) Never (3) Depends (4) Usually
(2) Seldom (5) Always

26. Does the situation described in #25 upset you?

(1) Yes, very much (3) Depends (4) Only a little
(2) Quite a bit (5) No, not at all

27. Helps you to develop skills in organizing materials.

(1) Never (3) Depends (4) Usually
(2) Seldom (5) Always

28. Does the situation described in #27 upset you?

(1) Yes, very much (3) Depends (4) Only a little
(2) Quite a bit (5) No, not at all

29. Understands you.

(1) Never (3) Depends (4) Usually
(2) Seldom (5) Always

30. Does the situation described in #29 upset you?

(1) Yes, very much (3) Depends (4) Only a little
(2) Quite a bit (5) No, not at all

31. Trusts you.

(1) Never (3) Depends (4) Usually
(2) Seldom (5) Always

32. Does the situation described in #31 upset you?

    (1) Yes, very much (3) Depends (4) Only a little
    (2) Quite a bit (5) No, not at all

33. Helps you to develop skills in making decisions.

    (1) Never (3) Depends (4) Usually
    (2) Seldom (5) Always

34. Does the situation described in #33 upset you?

    (1) Yes, very much (3) Depends (4) Only a little
    (2) Quite a bit (5) No, not at all

35. Helps you to develop skills in finding information.

    (1) Never (3) Depends (4) Usually
    (2) Seldom (5) Always

36. Does the situation described in #35 upset you?

    (1) Yes, very much (3) Depends (4) Only a little
    (2) Quite a bit (5) No, not at all

37. Helps you to develop skills in using time wisely.

    (1) Never (3) Depends (4) Usually
    (2) Seldom (5) Always

38. Does the situation described in #37 upset you?

    (1) Yes, very much (3) Depends (4) Only a little
    (2) Quite a bit (5) No, not at all

39. Encourages you.

    (1) Never (3) Depends (4) Usually
    (2) Seldom (5) Always

40. Does the situation described in #39 upset you?

    (1) Yes, very much (3) Depends (4) Only a little
    (2) Quite a bit (5) No, not at all

LISTENING AND ACCEPTING

Although this book is mainly devoted to questioning techniques, listening to students in a sincerely interested manner is an important component to the questioning process. Teachers should listen, not analyze, evaluate, or judge, but just listen, until the student has finished his answer to a question. Some instructors do not do this. They start to dissect critically what the student is saying before he has had a chance to finish. Remember that many students' ideas are good, but they suffer from poor verbalization. If you wait until a student finishes his answers before mentally reacting, you will more likely grasp the student's ideas and better convey in non-verbal ways that you are sincerely interested in his ideas. A European friend of ours once told us that the curse of Americans is they are too analytical. They constantly analyze but they don't really listen in an accepting way.

The accepting of all responses is another rule to follow in developing good questioning techniques. There are three ways the word *accept* may be used:

1. accept = agree
2. accept = understand
3. accept = understand your views, but don't necessarily condone them.

To most teachers, to accept means to agree and, as a consequence, they react with this view to the detriment of good questioning techniques. Teachers should truly value all answers and be less prone to make judgments. They should try to respond using the word accept as indicated in numbers two and three above as much as possible.

Teachers should avoid making judgments on and correcting faulty answers. Some educators believe that the emphasis on judging and correcting faulty responses of students is detrimental to the learning process. They argue that real learning occurs only when the student makes discoveries in his own mind. In such a process, the student devises tests to determine whether or not his judgments are correct, or later in the educational process he encounters additional information forcing him to correct faulty procedures. Whether these views are correct is open to argument. There are, however, many instances in which teachers have led discussions making no judgments and the students progressed through toward appropriate conclusions.

Mary Budd Rowe has found in analysis of teacher questioning procedures in class discussion that instructors often rush student responses.[5] Good answers, and above all, creative answers, take time. Give students time to think—silence is no crime! And, when that silence is filled with mental thought, it truly is an

[5] Mary Budd Rowe, "Science, Silence, and Sanctions," *Science and Children*, March, 1969, p. 11.

exciting educational environment. It seems reasonable, therefore, that teachers should talk less, judge less, listen more, and wait longer for responses.

A TEST ON THE RECOGNITION OF GOOD QUESTIONS

With this brief introduction behind you, now test yourself on your ability to identify good questions. Read all of the questions below, keeping in mind those you think are better than others. After reading them, pause for a few minutes and try to determine what makes some of these questions better than others. Then turn to the analysis sheet on pp. 17–19 and answer the questions.

1. Why do roots suck water?
2. What is two times two?
3. If you were going to repeat the experiment, how would you improve it?
4. What mental steps did you go through in solving this problem?
5. What are the implications of this novel for our time?
6. If you were mayor, what would you do to solve the ghetto problem?
7. If you are aggressive in an argument, how will the other group members react?
8. How should you behave in order to build the "self-concepts" of the people with whom you associate?
9. How should you act in order to build your "self-concept?"
10. What relevance do you think the material we are studying has for you?
11. What implications did the Hitler takeover have for our society?
12. When was Washington born?
13. How would you define a magnet operationally?
14. How could you be more certain of your conclusions?
15. What groups would you divide these into?
16. How would you go about solving this problem?
17. If you were going to design an experiment to determine the answer, what would you do?
18. What do you think will happen to a potted geranium plant if it is placed near a window?
19. What do you think will happen to the schools if bussing is stopped?

20. Do you think your answer is right?
21. What has happened to the number of accidents since the overpass was constructed?
22. How did the seed sprout?
23. Can cancer be cured?
24. If you have a straight line graph indicating a relationship between population growth and time but the period ends at two days, what could you say about the population at four days?
25. What evidence does the process of diffusion contribute to the molecular theory?
26. What strikes you about this painting?
27. What kinds of feelings does this music stimulate in you?
28. If you could create something what would it be?
29. How do you feel about that?

Analysis of the Above Questions

Read the following questions and attempt to answer them as best you can. Write the number of the questions you choose for answers under each of the questions below so that you can refer back to your answers later in the book. From time to time after reading one of the chapters, return to these questions and reread them—change any answers you wish, but do not erase the old ones so that you can compare how your questioning awareness is being modified because of your reading. If possible, compare your answers with another person or discuss them in groups.

Example: for question 1, you might choose 5, 7, and 9. You would then record your answers as indicated below:

1. "What three questions from the preceding list do you think are the best ones for a teacher to ask?"

   Your answers: 5, 7, 9.

Question Analysis List

1. What three questions from the preceding list do you think are the best ones for a teacher to ask?

   Your answers:

2. Which are teleological or anthropomorphic questions?

   Your answers:

3. Which questions require the student to analyze?

   Your answers:

4. Which questions require the student to synthesize?

   Your answers:

5. Which questions require the student to evaluate?

   Your answers:

6. Which questions are convergent?

   Your answers:

7. Which questions are divergent?

   Your answers:

8. Which questions require the student to demonstrate critical thinking in his response?

   Your answers:

9. What questions require creative responses?

   Your answers:

10. What questions require the student to formulate an operational definition?

    Your answers:

11. What questions require the student to formulate a model?

    Your answers:

12. Which questions require students to reason quantitatively and what are they required to do?

    Your answers:

13. What questions require a student mainly to observe?

    Your answers:

14. What questions require a student mainly to classify?

    Your answers:

15. What questions require a student to demonstrate experimental procedure?

    Your answers:

16. What questions require a student to hypothesize?

    Your answers:

17. Which questions would an authoritarian personality most likely guess at if he didn't know the answer?

    Your answers:

18. Which of the following two types of questions suggests a test?

    a. How do seeds sprout?
    b. What is needed for seeds to sprout?

    Your answers:

19. It has been said that "how" questions do not lead to experimentation. Comment on this below:

    Your answers:

20. How would you classify most of the above questions on this sheet?

    Your answers:

21. What other questions should this sheet contain?

    Your answers:

It should be noted that most of the above questions are fairly good. The sophistication of questioning will naturally vary with the mental age of students. However, some of the above questions allow for only a few possible answers—such as yes or no. (Which of the above questions can be answered by yes or no?) These questions are not necessarily bad, but you wouldn't want to start a discussion with them. Why? The answer to this question will be covered in considerable detail later in the book.

The Improvement of Your Questioning Ability Never Ends

American society is youth oriented. Our advertisements continually picture the young and beautiful—youth is esteemed and the aged tolerated. This is true with the exception of the wise. A wise man is always valued, admired, and respected as a model to which to aspire. An actively involved teacher continually striving for the improvement of his competence is on the road to wisdom. But wisdom does not come without much effort and modification of behavior. It is easy to read this book, but it is far more difficult to apply its message not only to your instructional behavior but your daily life as well. For, what we have to say about listening, acceptance, questioning, and building "self concepts" has relevance not only to teaching but to living as a wise person as well.

Behavior changes slowly and then only with effort. In order for you to become a wise questioner, you will have to want to change, work for change, and evaluate your progress. The joy of the book's message will come only when you apply its suggestions. The success you will have as a result should act as a stimulus to continue modification of your behavior toward becoming a better instructor and person. We wish you well on your road to wisdom, and invite any reactions you have from reading our book.

SUMMARY

It is our view that there is beginning in American education a rennaissance stressing the humanistic importance of the individual person. A human is a complex of talents which number in the hundreds. Schools have traditionally emphasized the manifestation of academic talent, but modern educators are becoming increasingly concerned with developing, valuing, and rewarding all of the human talents—the creative, quantifiable, social, organizonal, communicative, mechanical, musical, artistic, etc. It is through the development and valuing of a person's talent that a student builds his "self-concept." All instructors should assess how a student views himself—his self-esteem—for it is how a person sees himself that best predicts in what ways and how he will react. The task of a teacher is to help an individual build his self-esteem, but unfortunately, many instructors and schools historically have done the opposite. Questions have been suggested in this chapter for assessing a person's impression of "self." Teachers who build self-esteem and relate to students as persons are rated highly by them. In fact, students rate this quality far more important than academic preparation for a teacher.

A teacher sincerely interested in individuals must develop excellent questioning and, equally important, listening skills. Often, teachers are eager to analyze critically the answers students give during their responses. Such analytical behavior on the part of the instructor, however, interferes with true listening. Teachers should listen and accept all responses, be less prone to judge, and give more opportunities for students to judge their own answers.

The improvement of questioning and listening does not come easily. It is a lifetime chore but one, if done well, which contributes to becoming a better teacher and a better person. It is through such efforts that an instructor continues toward the path of wisdom leading to becoming a truly great teacher.

2

WHY IS QUESTIONING SO VITAL?

It is almost impossible to think of any specific teaching technique used more frequently by teachers than questioning. This fact has been substantiated by research on teaching behavior and classroom interaction by Edmund Amidon[1], Arno A. Bellack[2], B. O. Smith[3], and others. These investigators, in analyzing classroom procedures, found teachers use questioning orally or written in the following ways to:

1. Arouse interest and to motivate children to participate actively in the lesson.
2. Evaluate a student's preparation and to check his comprehension of homework or previous assignments.
3. Diagnose student's strengths and weaknesses.
4. Review and/or summarize what has been presented.
5. Encourage discussions.
6. Direct children to new possibilities in the problem being explored.
7. Stimulate students to seek out additional data on their own.
8. Build up an individual student's positive self-concept (making certain, however, that the student can respond adequately).

---

1 Edmund J. Amidon and John B. Hough (eds.), *Interaction Analysis: Theory, Research and Application* (Reading, Mass.: Addison-Wesley Publishing Co., Inc. (1967).

2 Arno A. Bellack, Herbert M. Kliebard, Ronald T. Hyman, Frank L. Smith, Jr., *The Language of the Classroom* (New York: Teachers College Press, 1966).

3 B. O. Smith, *Teachers for the Real World* (Washington, D.C.: The American Association of Colleges for Teacher Education, 1969).

9. Help children see applications for previously learned concepts.
10. Assess the degree of success in achieving the goals and objectives of his lesson.

By proper use of questions, the teacher structures his:

Subject matter . . . . WHAT to teach?
Teaching methods . . . . HOW to teach?
Sequence of teaching. . . . . WHEN to teach?

However, prior to these considerations are the teacher's view or philosophy of the purposes for his questions. What goals does the teacher have?

GOALS FOR MODERN EDUCATION

The work of Swiss psychologist Jean Piaget is profoundly affecting the direction of today's education. His contributions in the area of child growth and development have influenced educators in most curricular areas. Piaget concisely summarized the purposes of education in modern society in lectures at Cornell University in 1964 in this way:

> The principal goal of education is to create men who are capable of doing new things, not simply of repeating what other generations have done—men who are creative, inventive, and discoverers. The second goal of education is to form minds which can be critical, can verify, and not accept everything they are offered. The great danger today is of slogans, collective opinions, ready-made trends of thought. We have to be able to resist individually, to criticize, to distinguish between what is proven and what is not. So we need pupils who are active, who learn early to find out by themselves, partly by their own spontaneous activity and partly through material we set up for them; who learn early to tell what is verifiable and what is simply the first idea to come to them.[4]

Piaget's Suggested Educational Objectives

1. Develop creative thinking, not just memory
2. Encourage critical analysis
3. Stimulate active participation in learning

[4] R. E. Ripple and V. N. Rockcastle (eds.), *Piaget Rediscovered* (Ithaca, N.Y.: Cornell University Press, 1964), p. 5.

The following are some of the research that has been carried out to determine the affect of questioning on the above three educational objectives:

1. *Develop Critical Thinking, Not Just Memory*

   Aschner, M. J., "Asking Questions to Trigger Thinking," *NEA Journal, 50,* 1961: 44–46.

   Carner, R. L., "Levels of Questioning," *Education, 83,* 1963: 546–550.

   Hunkins, F. P., "Using Questions to Foster Pupil Thinking," *Education, 87,* 1966: 83–87.

   Witryol, S. L., "Discrimination learning, problem solving and choice patterning by children as a function of incentive, value, motivation, and sequential dependencies. Unpublished manuscript. Storrs: University of Connecticut, 1967.

2. *Encourage Critical Analysis*

   Davis, O. L. and D. C. Tinsley, "Cognitive Objectives Revealed by Classroom Questions by Social Studies Student Teachers," *Peabody Journal of Education, 45,* 1967: 21–26.

   Massialas, B. G. and C. B. Cox, *Inquiry in Social Studies* (New York: McGraw-Hill, 1966).

3. *Stimulate Active Participation in Learning*

   Bereiter, C. *Acceleration of Intellectual Development in Early Childhood* (Urbana: University of Illinois Press, June 1967).

   Pate, R. T. and N. H. Bremer, "Guiding Learning Through Skillful Questioning," *Elementary School Journal, 67,* 1967: 417–422.

MEMORY AND HIGHER THINKING QUESTIONS

Benjamin S. Bloom and his associates edited the now classic books[5], in which they developed a system for classifying educational objectives. Bloom's purpose was to devise a system so that any educational objective could be classified within one of three domains:

---

[5] Benjamin S. Bloom (Ed.), *Taxonomy of Education Objectives* (New York: David McKay Company, 1956); and David R. Krathwohl, Benjamin S. Bloom, and Bertram B. Masia, *Taxonomy of Educational Objectives: Handbook II: Affective Domain* (New York: David McKay Company, 1964).

Bloom's Categories	*Aspect of Education Involved*
Cognitive Domain.....	intellectual (recall of knowledge)
Affective Domain......	emotional (interest, attitudes, values)
Psychomator Domain..	physical (manipulation and motor skills)

Within each domain, Bloom defined a number of categories of thinking. These categories are arranged in a hierarchy by Bloom, who also states that these categories of thinking are cumulative. A sequential and cumulative system of classifying is called a *taxonomy,* which means that, although each category has its own unique features, it also includes some elements of all lower categories. The following chart[6] is presented to illustrate the sequential and cumulative aspects:

Bloom's Taxonomy of Educational Objectives

Cognitive Domain

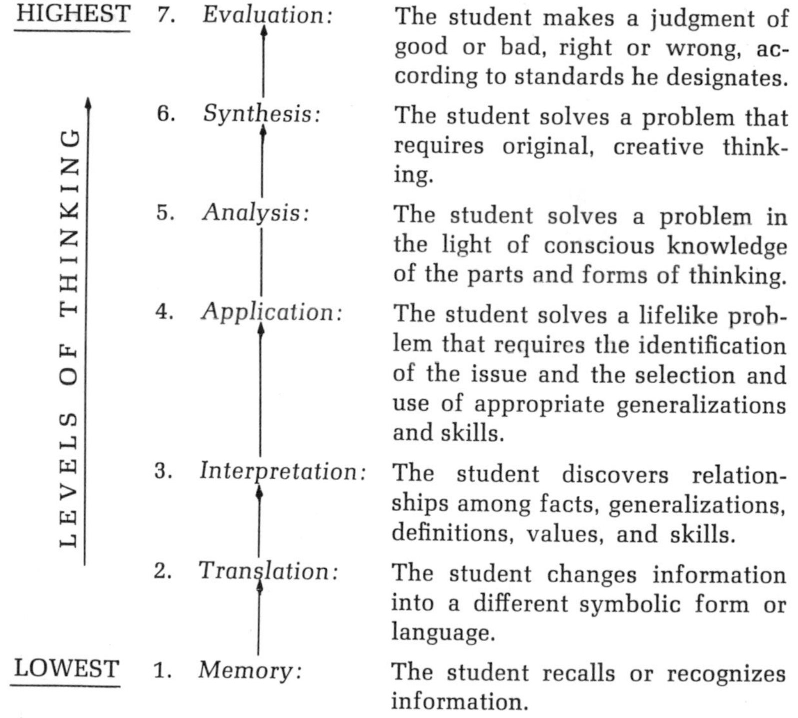

[6] Data from *Classroom Questions: What Kinds?* by Norris M. Sanders (Harper and Row, 1966), pp. 3 and 10.

It is obvious that levels of questions can be devised for Bloom's Taxonomy of Educational Objectives. Chapters 4 and 5 will deal with specific suggestions for writing questions for the cognitive and affective domains.

Importance of memory

From an examination of the above chart, it is evident that memory is the *only* thought process upon which all other kinds of thinking is based. Robert Gagné emphasizes the need for acquiring broad, generalized knowledge (lower level thinking which is primarily memory) before moving on to higher thinking levels. The transition between the theories of Bloom and Gagné follows:

1. Discovery learning can be undertaken only after the individual has acquired a store of broad and critical knowledge, and this, in turn, can be acquired only when he has learned some prerequisite but very fundamental capabilities.
2. At the earliest levels of instruction, the individual needs to learn these prerequisites: how to observe, how to figure, how to measure, how to orient things in space, how to describe, how to classify objects and events, how to infer, and how to make conceptual models.
3. These prerequisites make possible the acquiring of broad knowledge of principles, the incisive knowledge which makes possible the self-criticism of new ideas.[7]

Although the memory level of thinking is basic to all higher thinking processes, the research shows overwhelmingly that teachers use memory questions in over 70 percent of their teaching time.[8] It was also found that teachers overemphasize *fact* questions in their examinations.[9] An analysis of questions used

[7] Robert M. Gagne, "The Learning Requirements for Enquiry," *Journal of Research in Science Teaching, 1* (1963), pp. 144–153.

[8] R. L. Carner, "Levels of Questioning," *Education*, 1963, pp. 83, 546–550; O. L. Davis and D. C. Tinsley, "Cognitive Objectives Revealed by Classroom Questions Asked by Social Studies Student Teachers," *Peabody Journal of Education*, 1967, pp. 45, 21–26: F. J. Guszak, "Teacher Questioning and Reading," *The Reading Teacher*, 1967, pp. 21, 227–234; and Hilda Taba, *Teaching Strategies and Cognitive Function in Elementary School Children*, U.S.O.E. Cooperative Research Project No. 2424, San Francisco State College, 1966.

[9] L. Pfeiffer and O. L. Davis, "Teacher-made Examinations: What Kind of Thinking Do They Demand?" *National Association For Secondary School Principals Bulletin*, 1965, pp. 1–10, 49.

in textbooks also revealed that memory or fact questions are predominantly used there.[10]

Raising children's levels of thinking

One of the goals of education is to teach the learner to learn. This level of thinking has been called learning by *discovery* or *inquiry.* Discovery or inquiry help the learner acquire knowledge which is uniquely his own because he discovered it for himself. Discovery or inquiry is not restricted to finding something entirely new to man, but encompasses all kinds of knowledge obtained by the use of one's own mind. It involves rearranging data internally in such a manner that the learner can go beyond the immediate situation to form new concepts. It means finding the meanings, organization, and structure of ideas.

This system of learning to learn is also referred to as *heuristics,* with its roots in ancient Greece. Legend has it that Archimedes shrieked, "*Eureka*" (meaning "I've found it!") when he discovered the percentage of gold in Heiro's crown.

Socrates (470–399 B.C.) is called the father of heuristics, because he used questioning to lead the learner to new "discoveries." He rejected the lecture method of teaching because he said that it put "ready-made" ideas in his student's minds. Socrates believed the *question* was the means of inducing thinking and thereby leading the student to discover his own wisdom. This point is emphasized in the graph below, where the learner's higher thinking processes closely follow the kinds of questions asked by their teachers. James Gallagher's studies show that even a *slight* increase in the percentage of teacher higher-thinking-type questions (called *divergent questions* by Gallagher) yields a *large* increase in divergent production by students. Such a question as, "What would happen if the United States had been colonized from the *west* coast to the east instead of vice versa?" can bring forth as many as fifteen or twenty responses, each related to divergent production on the part of students.[11]

[10] F. D. Curtis, "Types of Thought Questions in Textbooks of Science," *Science Education,* 1943, pp. 24, 60–67; *and* O. L. Davis and F. P. Hunkins, "Textbook Questions: What Thinking Processes Do They Foster?" *Peabody Journal of Education,* 1966, pp. 43, 285–292.

[11] James J. Gallagher and Mary Jane Aschner, "A Preliminary Report on Classroom Interaction," *Merrill-Palmer Quarterly of Behavior and Development,* 9, July 1963, pp. 183, 194. Reprinted by permission of author and publisher.

Relation of Teacher Questions to Student Divergent Thinking Production[12]

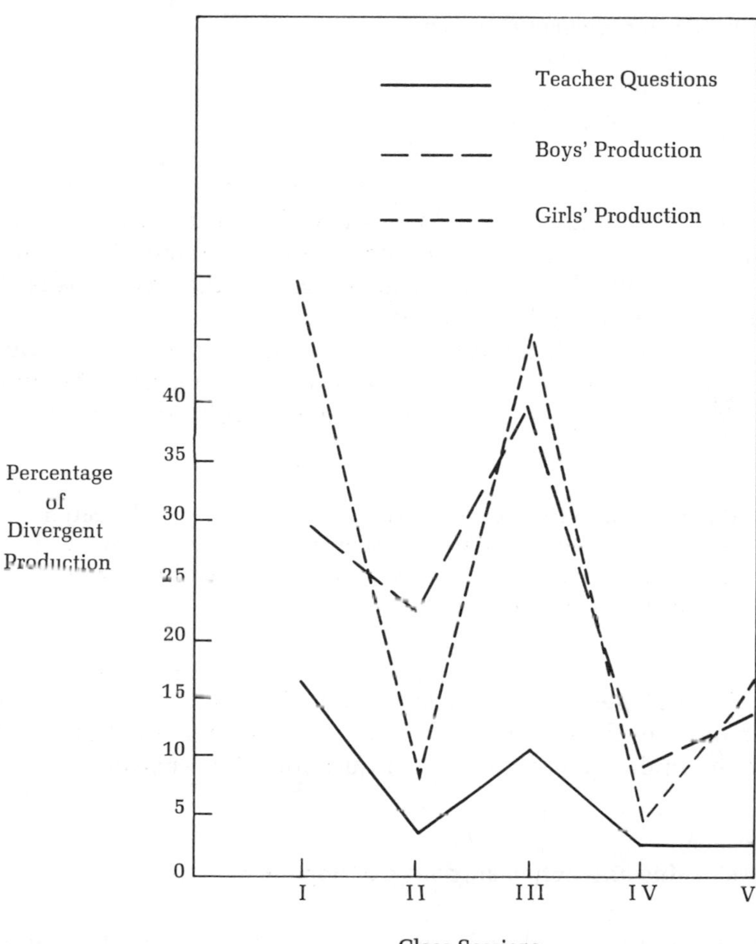

Discovery learning

The importance of learning by discovery or heuristics and the importance of the role of proper questioning in it have been advanced by such educational leaders as Jean Piaget, Jerome Bruner,

---

[12] Ibid.

and Richard Suchman. Bruner, a Harvard University psychologist, lists the benefits of discovery teaching-learning as follows:

1. Greater intellectual potency
2. Intrinsic motivation
3. Memory processing
4. The learning of the heuristics of discovery[13]

In *Learning By Discovery,* edited by Lee Shulman and Evan Keislar, outstanding psychologists and educators provide critical analyses of current assertions and research about the value of discovery methods in teaching-learning. It is their consensus that more critical research is needed.

M. C. Wittrock, an author of one of the chapters in the book, "The Learning By Discovery Hypotheses," summarizes the apparent advantage of teaching-learning higher thinking processes as follows:

> When the criterion is the learning of concepts and hierarchically ordered subject matter, discovery may fare better. If the criteria are transferred to new concepts, originality, and learning by discovery, learning by discovery as a treatment may fare well.[14]

Both Piaget and Bruner emphasize the urgency for *active* participation by the learner in the teaching-learning situation and for improving the quality of *student* questions and answers.

Questioning and active student participation

Teacher questions must be used to actively involve the learner. To increase pupil participation, the following teacher questioning techniques are suggested.[15]

---

[13] Jerome S. Bruner, "The Act of Discovery," *Harvard Education Review, 31,* 1961, pp. 21–34, 54, 140, 148.

[14] M. C. Wittrock, "The Learning By Discovery Hypothesis" in Lee S. Shulman and Evan R. Keislar (eds.), *Learning By Discovery* (Chicago, Ill.: Rand McNally and Co., 1966), p. 73.

[15] The following discussion draws heavily on these references: Minicourse: *Effective Questioning—Elementary Level, Teachers Handbook* by Walter R. Borg, Marjorie L. Kelly, and Philip Langer by permission of Macmillan

1. Pose *"group-oriented"* questions instead of directing a question to one person. Ask your question, pause briefly, and then call upon student.

   Poor: "Alice, have scientists actually seen electrons?"

   Better: "What factors should you consider when selecting a college? *[Pause]* Alice?"

   Advantages of group-oriented questions are:

   a. Keeps students alert and thinking
   b. Broadens participation by inviting several students to show their readiness to answer.

It goes without saying that there are times when the teacher *deliberately* calls upon only one student before asking his question. These situations lend themselves to teacher directing his question to a particular student:

a. As a way to get the attention of a student who is inattentive.
b. When a student is drifting out of the discussion, the teacher might pose this question:

   "*Larry*, How would *you* rephrase the answer into your own words?"
c. If the teacher wishes to call upon the same student who has given a previous answer, in order to modify, expand, or correct his answer.
d. To draw a shy student who is easily upset or startled into the discussion. The student *may* feel better if the teacher asks:

   "Michael, how would you summarize why some students in our class called the Bay of Pigs "Kennedy's fiasco"?"

   or

   "Johnny, what was your reaction to Sally's statement that dope addicts should be hospitalized and not jailed?"

Educational Services, Inc. © Copyright 1970 by the Far West Laboratory for Educational Research and Development; Philip Groisser, *How to Use the Fine Art of Questioning* (New York: Teachers Practical Press, 1964); R. L. Loughlin, "On Questioning," *The Educational Forum,* 1961, pp. 25, 481–482. Used by permission of Kappa Delta Pi, An Honor Society in Education, owners of the copyright.

2. Avoid "chorus-type" convergent questions encouraging the class to respond en masse. Such questions may take such form as:

   "Did the United States ever wage a war against Canada, class?"

   or

   "Class, who is President Nixon's Vice-President?"

The resulting simultaneous calling out of answers to these questions may weaken classroom discipline or decorum, contribute to anonymity of students, lack of responsibility for correct answers, indefiniteness of answers, as well as requiring the teacher to repeat the question for an answer by *one* student.

3. Ask questions of as wide a range of students as possible. Students who are involved in class discussions are more likely to be *actively* involved in the teaching-learning processes than students who sit quietly and do not participate.

Call upon *non-volunteers* as well as volunteers, depending upon the situation. Allowing non-participants to remain silent reinforces that behavior. The following are some of the times when it is better for a teacher *not* to call upon non-volunteers or to pursue unduly an answer:

a. If a student has a severe speech or language handicap.
b. If the student has been absent for a prolonged period and does not possess the needed background information.

In such cases, the teacher must select the appropriate time and questions to suit the situation. Follow-up work should be done by the teacher with the student's parents, school psychologist, principal, and/or guidance counsellor.

If handled carefully, calling on non-volunteers or non-contributors in class discussion may have these salutary effects:

a. Shy students may be assisted in "breaking the ice" and encouraged through success to try it again.
b. The teacher can ascertain strengths and weaknesses of non-volunteers and build upon these for future teaching-learning activities.

c. Bright students may hesitate to volunteer for social reasons and can be gently encouraged by a direct question.

4. Questions should be adjusted to the language and conceptual level of the students. Wording of questions should be carefully thought out. These examples show how appropriate selections of words may be utilized:

Average or Bright Group	*Slower Group*
labor force	workers
bourgeoisie	middle class
nouveau riche	new rich
apparatus	equipment
management	boss

The same consideration should be given to the difficulty level of the concepts being sought:

Average or Bright Group	*Slower Group*
Explain the phrase, "balance of nature."	What effect do birds have on the insect population?
What is the role of symbolism in the author's character selection?	Why did the author pick the different kinds of people in his book?
How did the Vietnam War develop a new brand of international isolationism among groups of young people in America?	Why are some young people today against the United States "getting involved" in Vietnam?

5. The way a teacher *handles student answers* may well be as important as the questions he asks. Four broad types of student answers are correct, incorrect, partially correct, and no answer at all. Some suggestions for handling each are:

Correct answers

The teacher may respond in some way by verbal comment or praise ("Excellent!" "Good!" "That's correct!" etc.), or occasionally non-verbally (a nod, pat on back, wink, etc.). A teacher responding to a student's correct answer performs these important functions:

1. Gives immediate feedback to the student that he's right. (*Reinforcement for learning*)
2. Sets an atmosphere showing that the teacher cares about the answers and will listen and respond. (*Encourages further or continued student participation.*) The teacher may wish to direct the class' attention to some aspect of the student's answer, such as:

   "Why does Bob's answer show that he's really sensitive to the feelings of oppressed people?"

   or

   "Which of Harry's points made the most sense to YOU?"

Incorrect answers

Incorrect answers require diplomatic handling, for the teacher must:

1. respond to the student
2. redirect the direction of thinking
3. move toward correct response
4. be careful of setting negative feelings into action which could block communication and learning
5. accept all answers

Without being punitive or belligerent, the teacher can accomplish his goals by following the acknowledgment of the student's incorrect answer by asking:

> "That's good thinking, Bob, but you didn't hit the bullseye. Who can help clarify Bob's answer?"
>
> "My question may have thrown you off. Let me ask it this way . . . "
>
> "Let's go back to our text to check those statistics. They are inaccurate. Bruce, on what page did you get them?"

> "Claire, I think you may confuse alliteration with onamonopia. I do that myself sometimes. Who can help *us* with a good example of each?"

For many students, especially slower ones, it is valuable to tell them you'll come back to them later. This gives them time to find correct answers and save face, as well as to develop responsibility for correcting their own answers.

Sometimes a pupil responds to the question asked with an irrelevant answer. This may be intentional or the student may have misunderstood the question. The teacher should redirect the question often with good humor, by saying:

> "Great Answer! Too bad it isn't appropriate for the question I asked. Perhaps I didn't state it well."
>
> "Let me state my question a bit differently."
>
> "You've gone beyond my question, Terry. Great, but hold the last part until we get to it later. OK?"

Because they may be very damaging to a student's self-concept and his subsequent learning, teachers should *avoid* the following types of responses to incorrect answers:

1. *Sarcasm.* Most children cannot fully appreciate the substance and feel only the barbs and hurts.
2. *Reprimand.* ("Write the correct answer one hundred times.") The negative carry-over to the subject matter being studied can be quite damaging.
3. *Personal attack.* ("Boy—are you stupid!") Children tend to function on the level the teacher sets for them.
4. *Accusative.* ("You didn't study that, did you?") Besides you may be inaccurate in your accusation.
5. *No response at all.* At least say: "I enjoyed your thinking." When the teacher does not respond to a student's answer, it is not only rude, it conveys a negative connotation. It also tends to make the student feel as if his contribution is worthless.

Partially correct answers

Very often students' answers lack something to make them completely correct. The teacher should handle such incomplete answers in one of the following ways:

1. Acknowledge and give credit for the correct part of the answer. Ask:

   "Your answer's correct, John, up to the point where you said . . . "

   or

   "I agree with you on your first point; however . . . "

   (This kind of teacher response gives the student a very positive feeling of worth and contribution.)

2. Try to have the incorrect or weak part of the student's answer improved. Ask:

   "What's your reaction to Barry's last statement that . . . "

   or

   "Tony, you almost have it. Great! How could you reword the second half of your answer to make it completely right?"

   or

   "Stephanie's answer is about 85 percent accurate. Can anyone spot her slight error?"

   or

   "How can Paula's answer be revised a bit to improve the part about . . . "

3. If the teacher wishes to correct misused or incorrect grammar (except in English or speech classes, of course), he should do so *unobtrusively* so as not to hinder the discussion. Allow student to finish his thought before inserting the correct usage.

   Student: "England and America *was* called the Allies in W.W. II."

   Teacher: "Correct—England and America *were* called the Allies in W.W. II."

   (By bringing the class' attention to the incorrect part of the answer, the teacher sets high [but realistic] standards; in addition, she non-punitively helps the student and class correct their own inperfections. The teacher also helps create an atmosphere for continual self-evaluation.)

No answer at all

Occasionally a teacher's question is greeted with no response by either volunteers or non-volunteers. The alert teacher can handle such a situation by:

1. Rephrasing the question on a simpler level, as the silence may be due to lack of clarity or stimulation of the original question. Ask:

   "Let me ask that question again in this way . . . "

2. If the reworded question fails to arouse student responses, the teacher might present more information by telling, showing a film, directing students to textbooks or previous assignments, etc. Then ask:

   "Now that we understand more about the basic functions of arteries and veins, who would like to try to tackle my original question about . . . ?"

SUMMARY

Questioning is used more frequently by teachers than any other single teaching technique. The goals of modern education are to develop creative thinking, encourage critical analysis, and involve the learner actively in the teaching-learning situation for his personal development and a positive self-concept.

Benjamin Bloom has devised a system for classifying these goals into three categories: cognitive (intellectual), affective (emotional), and psychomotor (manipulative). Jerome Bruner, among other educators, suggests that students must be helped to learn by discovery. In the process of doing this, they will develop Bloom's higher cognitive levels of thinking. Practical suggestions are presented for actively involving the learner and for improving teacher questioning techniques.

3

DEVELOPING STUDENT QUESTIONING AND DISCUSSION SKILLS

Chapter 2 focussed upon the *teacher's* role in stimulating and directing student participation in discussions through questioning. This chapter focuses upon the improvement of the *student's* questioning and discussion skills as a necessary requirement for discovery or higher cognitive inquiry learning.

STUDENTS' QUESTIONS AND DISCUSSIONS

Active involvement of the learner is essential for developing his skills in the higher cognitive levels of thinking. Several research projects have found that higher levels of thinking are best obtained when students are encouraged to:

1. Develop skill in asking their *own* questions in seeking solutions to problems
2. Participate more in *pupil-pupil* discussions than teacher-pupil ones

Developing student questioning skills

One of the goals of discovery learning is to help students become self-learners. Richard Suchman and his associates at the University of Illinois designed a program which stressed improving *student* questioning as a tool for self-learning. In his Inquiry Development Program (IDP)[1], Suchman views students mentally

---

[1] For additional information, the reader should consult J. Richard Suchman, *Developing Inquiry* (Chicago: Science Research Associates, Inc., 1966).

organizing data from facts to theories to applications. Although IDP used science content only, the approach is applicable to *all* subject matter fields.

In the diagram below, discovery learning of facts to theories to applications occurs in *horizontal* channels. Memory or rote learning occurs in *vertical* channels. IDP tried to develop student skills so that they would move away from teacher-dominated learning (vertical) to greater student-dominated learning (horizontal).

Suchman's Communications Diagram[2]

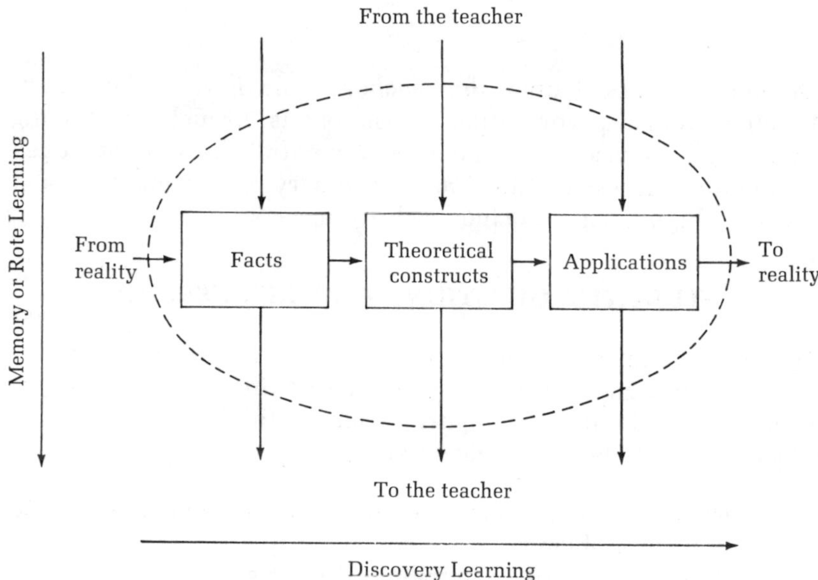

Here are some suggestions from IDP findings to assist teachers of *all* subjects who wish to try "inquiry sessions" to improve their students' questions and self-learning:

1. Present a "problem episode" to the class giving as much factual material as needed but which does not give teacher opinion or bias. In IDP *silent* film episodes of

[2] Diagram modified by the authors from Robert B. Davis, "Discovery in the Teaching of Mathematics," in Lee S. Shulman and Evan R. Keislar (eds.), *Learning by Discovery*, © 1966 by Rand McNally and Co., Chicago, p. 125.

physical events are presented without captions or comments from the teacher, such as a pitcher throwing a curve ball, boiling water by cooling it, etc.

2. Ask students to offer theories or hunches to account for their observations of the facts.
3. After all theories are proposed by students, encourage them to ask *you* questions to test the theories presented. Some ground rules should be established during this phase of the inquiry session, perhaps along these lines suggested by the IDP studies:[3]
   a. The questions should be phrased in such a way that they can be answered yes or no.
   b. Once called upon, a student may ask as many questions as he or she wishes before yielding the floor.
   c. The teacher does not answer yes or no to statements of theories or to questions that attempt to obtain the teacher's approval of a theory.
   d. Any student can test any theory at any time.
   e. Any time the students feel a need to converse with one another without the teacher's presence, they should be free to call a conference.
   f. Students should be able to refer to resource books, kits of materials or any other source of information at any time they feel the need.
4. Tape record the inquiry sessions, which may range in time from ten minutes to an hour depending upon children's backgrounds, topic explored, and students' experience with this novel approach.
5. Students should refine their theories about the problem episode from the teacher's responses to their questions.
6. Students and teachers cooperatively analyze students' questions and the kinds of data they produced. This can best be done by replaying the tape recording made of the questioning session.
7. Assist students in evaluating productive and frivolous questions. Help them to see questions that aided or hindered finding relationships between elements in their problem episode.

---

[3] J. Richard Suchman, *Putting Inquiry Into Science: Learning Development Program* (Chicago: Science Research Associates, Inc., 1966), p. 4.

8. Guide a final practice time when students apply what has been learned to systematically arriving at more meaningful explanations of their problem episodes.

The following is a portion of an actual inquiry session in a suburban sixth grade.[4] The problem episode was a silent film depicting the heating of a bi-metallic knife. The knife blade first curls in one direction when heated and then curls the other way when cooled. The teacher opens the questioning session with an invitation:

Student Questions and Teacher Responses	*Teacher's Thinking*
T: O.K., any theories? Bill?	Invitation to theorize first. Children have ideas about "why" well before they feel ready to gather data. Theories give purpose and direction to data gathering.
B: Was the knife made out of copper?	An attack on the blade to find out what it's made of, which may give a clue. No telling why he picked copper first.
T: Partly.	This gives something away, but it is an honest answer.
B: Was it an alloy of any sort?	
T: Yes.	
B: Was it something with copper and tungsten maybe?	
T: No.	
B: Well, in that basin, was it chemical or water?	What does Bill mean by "chemical"? Isn't water a chemical? Apparently not to him. There's a temptation to correct him, but why do so at this point? It is clear what he wants to know, and that's the most important thing. If it's water, he knows most of its properties. If it's something else, he'll have to learn more about its properties. The liquid could be crucial, and
T: You mean something different from water? You could call water a chemical too, I should think.	
B: Yeah.	
T: Well, do you want to ask me about one or the other?	

[4] J. Richard Suchman, *Developing Inquiry* (Chicago: Science Research Associates, Inc., 1966), pp. 35–36. By permission of publisher.

Student Questions and Teacher Responses	*Teacher's Thinking*
	his future strategy depends upon the answer to this question.
B: Is it water?	Once he determines that it is water, he can turn his attention elsewhere. He passes to think for awhile.
T: Yes.	
B: I pass.	
T: David.	
D: Is it supposed to be copper, or since the blade is partly copper, would the other be sulfur? Not sulphur, but—yeah, sulfur.	

. . . .

Students (and teachers too) may find reversing the "usual" roles of teacher-asking and students-responding a bit strange at first. However, much value is found in putting the learner in the position of *actively* pushing the teacher for pertinent data for finding answers to the problem episode. The following techniques have been successfully used by teachers in inquiry or student-questioning sessions:

1. Encourage *all* students to propose theories and questions.
2. Be prepared to *accept* all theories and questions *without value judgements,* no matter how "far out" they may be.
3. If, in the teacher's opinion, the student's question seems too far off the topic or too difficult for the majority of the class, the teacher could invite the student to discuss it privately after class.
4. Should the student's question require additional explanation, the teacher should direct it to the class before responding to it himself, by saying:

   "Can anyone answer Sidney's question?"

   or

   "Who thinks he can give us additional information for Ida's sharp question?"
5. Good questions should be praised and directed to the class for discussion, saying: "Excellent question, Juan, let's see who is tuned in and can answer it."

6. If the student's question cannot be answered immediately, the question maker and the class should be directed to hunt up data for the next day's discussion.

More pupil-pupil discussions

Another important element in encouraging students to participate more actively in learning is to focus upon the *direction* of classroom discussion. Too often the direction is only teacher-to-student-to-teacher. W. D. Floyd tape recorded 31 one-hour class sessions in elementary schools. His word count of teacher and pupil talk showed that 71 per cent of all words spoken were by the teacher.[5] Only occasionally did teachers encourage and stimulate students to discuss and interact with many other students in the class. Robert Karplus advocates these virtues of increased pupil-to-pupil dialogue:

> This pupil-pupil interaction, which occurs when children have common experiences and can discuss them among themselves, is most important in the children's intellectual development. Justifying a position or disagreeing with one's peers causes the individual to reconsider and re-evaluate his own decisions.[6]

In addition to the above virtues of encouraging *pupil-pupil* interaction are these:

1. Tends to produce more sustained variety and enriched responses both from individual and from a greater diversity of children.
2. Stimulates volunteering by more students.
3. Contributes to more group cooperation.
4. Approaches a more realistic social situation.
5. Minimizes the tendency toward teacher-dominated lessons.
6. Places burden for *active* learning upon student rather than over-dependence upon teacher.
7. Increases flow of ideas and avoids fragmenting discussion.

---

[5] W. D. Floyd, "An Analysis of the Oral Questioning Activity in Selected Colorado Primary Classrooms." Unpublished doctoral dissertation, Colorado State College, 1960.

[6] Robert Karplus and Herbert D. Thier, *A New Look at Elementary School Science—Science Curriculum Improvement Study* (Chicago: Rand McNally and Co., 1967), p. 65.

Some suggestions for increasing pupil-pupil interaction in using questioning in discussions are:

1. Improve the *physical* environment to maximize student interaction:
   a. Arrange furniture so students are face-to-face in a circle, horseshoe, etc.
   b. Seat students close enough to each other so that they don't have to squint or raise their voices.
   c. Provide comfortable temperature, lighting, etc.
   d. Provide audio-visual, laboratory, or other needed equipment and materials, and check them in advance to insure proper functioning.
   e. Library and other reading resources should be available to provide opportunity to temporarily suspend discussion to check facts or acquire additional data.
2. Assist students to see the significance of the discussion by tying it up to the work in class and its relation to their lives.
3. Early in the discussion, orally and on the chalkboard, pose questions that clarify the issues to be discussed. You might ask:

   "Be prepared to take a position on the Scopes Trial and defend it."

   or

   "Should pollution remedies be paid for by government or private sources?"

   or

   "Is automation a curse or blessing?"
4. Plan questions to guide and move discussion along, as well as to provide cohesiveness. This may be done by teacher by keeping these things in mind:
   a. Refrain from talking as long as discussion moves freely and productively.
   b. Enter discussion when you feel a balance is needed in the pros and cons by asking:

      "Tom, would you care to respond to Joe's point?"
   c. When summary is needed you could ask:

      "Clarence, please go to the chalkboard and list the points that we made so far."

d. Observe and point out the need for more data or greater clarification of some point, by asking:

"We seem to need more information on this. Don't you agree we could stop for now and bring in the material on osmosis tomorrow?"

e. Introduce new arguments or viewpoints if discussion stalls by asking:

"How could another military commitment like Vietnam be prevented?"

5. Sense the proper time to conclude and summarize discussion before class ends by asking:

"Since we're limited in time, let's see if we can summarize our conclusions in the next ten minutes."

or

"Let's see where we are. Claudia, will you summarize the pro arguments and will David do the same for the con side?"

6. Help students to learn how to differ politely with one another by examining their feelings caused by these different expressions.

Negative Expressions	*Positive Expressions*
"You're all wet!"	"I see a contradiction in . . . "
"Your facts are all wrong."	"My text says . . . "
"You seem all mixed up."	"I disagree with Jon because . . . "

Two additional suggestions warrant somewhat expanded explanations: wait-time and reward and punishments.

Wait-Time

The amount of time that elapses between a teacher asking a question and calling upon a student to answer that question is called "wait-time." The average teacher's wait-time is *one second!* Mary Budd Rowe, Columbia University science educator, reports these gains when the teachers in her research project increased their wait-time:

Student Responses Lengthen

1. If you can prolong your average "wait-time" to five seconds or longer, the length of student responses increases. When wait-time is very short, students tend to give very short answers or they are prone to say, "I don't know." In addition, their answers often come with a question mark in the tone, as if to say, "Is this what you want?"

Whole Sentences

2. . . . you are more likely to get whole sentences, and the confidence as expressed by tone is higher.

Speculative Thinking

3. Another bonus that results from increased wait-times is the appearance of speculative thinking (e.g., "It might be the water," . . . "but it could be too many plants.") and the use of arguments based on evidence.

Shift to Child-Child Behaviors

4. If the wait-time is prolonged an average of five seconds or more, young children shift from teacher-centered show-and-tell kinds of behavior to child-child comparing of differences.

Children's Questions Increase

5. As you increase the wait-time, the number of questions children ask and the number of experiments they need to answer the questions multiply.

Teacher's Flexibility Increases

6. . . . By increasing the wait-time, you buy for yourself an opportunity to hear and to think.

Teachers Revise Their Expectations of Children

7. . . . Wait-time can change your expectations about what some children can do. (Before teachers increased their wait-times, students rated as slow or less apt by teachers had to try to answer questions more rapidly than students rated as bright or fast.)

Teachers Increase Their Variety of Questions

8. . . . As wait-time increases, teachers begin to show much more variability in the kinds of questions they ask. Students get more opportunity to respond to thought rather than straight memory questions."[7]

In summary, an increase in teacher wait-time sets an atmosphere more conducive to productive questions on higher thinking levels. Students use the wait-time to organize more complete answers. To assist you in using wait-time more effectively, the following suggestions are presented:

---

[7] Mary Budd Rowe, "Science, Silence, and Sanctions," *Science and Children*, March, 1969, pp. 12–13. Reproduced with permission from *Science and Children*, March, 1969. Copyright 1969 by the National Science Teachers Association, 1201 Sixteenth Street, N.W., Washington, D.C. 20036.

1. Increase *your* wait-time to 5 seconds or longer if needed.
2. Immediately before or after you ask a question, set the stage for your students to give careful thought to their answer. You might say:

   "I've asked a difficult question, so take your time in thinking about it."

   or

   "When I call on you, please give me a complete answer."

   or

   "My next question is very complex. Please give it your thoughtful consideration."
3. Become aware of how long *you* wait for *particular* students to respond after your question. *Consciously* focus upon increasing your wait-time for "slow" or shy students.
4. Caution children not to call out answers during the increased wait-time. You might say:

   "Let's all be silent now so *everyone* has the chance to think about the question."

   or

   "Some of us are not able to think about the question, because of all the calling out. Please respect your neighbors' right to quiet during this time."

   or

   "I know you're anxious to share your answer, but give those who haven't finished thinking about their answer a chance."
5. Avoid asking questions at so rapid a rate that you feel compelled to answer them to move things along.

   "What president was Lincoln? Number 16 wasn't he?"
6. Include types of questions that call upon higher cognitive skills than merely rapid-fire memory questions.

Rewards and punishments

If teachers are to help children engage in higher cognitive thinking activities, they must evaluate their interpersonal relationships as well as their teaching methods. Ronald Hyman, in his thorough research of teaching styles, put it this way:

> . . . if the activity is to be called teaching, the teacher must respect the student, must seek to minimize anxiety and threat, and must seek to establish mutual trust. . . . But to be called teaching, the activity must involve this positive interpersonal relationship to some degree that promotes learning and the development of the independence of the student.[8]

To put it another way, the sanctions of the teacher (rewards and punishments) during questioning and discussion affect how his students learn. In Chapter 2, "Why Is Questioning So Vital?" suggestions were presented for responding to student's correct, incorrect, partially correct, and no-answer-at-all answers. Inherent in all of the teacher's responses to these student answers is reward and punishment.

The emphasis in criticism should be upon the student's *response,* not upon *him,* even though all students respond personally to criticism. Research shows not only many short-range bad side effects of using punishment, but also these long-lasting effects:

1. Punishment does not necessarily eradicate undesirable pupil behavior. Under certain circumstances, once punishment is withdrawn, the behavior will be repeated.
2. Punishment often generates emotional reactions (including anxiety, fear, hate, etc.) which has long lasting consequences. These emotional responses are likely to be associated with the teacher, classroom, and/or the entire learning situation. Subsequently, the student may display behavior ranging from refusing to answer questions and sulking, to skipping class and outright defiance of the teacher.
3. The student will also do things which serve to reduce the future possibility of punishment. For example, if he is punished for an incorrect answer to a question, the pupil may subsequently refuse to volunteer in class.[9]

Although teachers are familiar with the above possible side effects of punishments, they may not be aware that rewards also present potential barriers to learning. Mary Budd Rowe has found

[8] Ronald T. Hyman, *Ways of Teaching* (New York: J. B. Lippincott Co., 1970), p. 19.

[9] Borg, et al., op. cit., pp. 33–34.

that "There is some reason to suspect that when children work on a complex task, rewards given by the teacher may interfere with logical thought processes. When children start attending to the reward rather than the task, the incidence of error or the necessity to repeat steps increases."[10]

The following suggestions are presented to aid teachers in balancing the use of sanctions in their question and answer periods.

1. Become aware of the ways in which your students respond to your use of reward and punishment.
2. When telling a student his answer is incorrect or partially correct, encourage him to try again to answer the question fully.
3. If you can determine which part of his answer is correct, praise that part and ask student to rethink the incorrect part. You might say:

   "You were right that Rogers and Hammerstein wrote Oklahoma, but let's look at the list of stars you say were in the *original* cast. What about Robert Goulet?"
4. Try to avoid *all* negative responses to student's answers even if they are incorrect. Instead use such techniques as:[11]

   a. *Probing* (a series of teacher questions addressed to one student and designed to move the student's initial response toward a more adequate answer)

Negative	*Positive*
"Your answer is wrong, Tom."	"Let's take a look at your answer, Tom."

   b. *Prompting* (a series of hints, used to help a pupil who gives a weak or incorrect answer)

      1. When there is no student response to question—rephrase question.

Question too vague	*Question more direct*
"How do you feel about religion?"	"What values does religion have for some people?"

---

[10] Mary Budd Rowe, op. cit., p. 13.

[11] For an expanded presentation of these points see Walter R. Borg, et al., op. cit., pp. 68–71.

2. When student needs returning to simpler materials:

Complex Question	*Simpler Question*
"What happened at Boston Tea Party?" "Why did it make England angry?"	"Why did they call it Boston *Tea* Party?"

c. *Seeking Further Clarification*
(used when the teacher wants to expand partial answer)

"What else can be added to your answer, Al?"
"How can you make yourself better understood?"
"Can you tell me why you believe that?"

d. *Refocusing*
(asking students to relate a wrong answer to another topic)

"How do you justify this answer with yesterday's discussion of . . . ?"

5. Ask students to use the results of their experiments to check the authenticity of their answers. This changes the focus of authority and need for sanction from teacher to observed data.
6. Learn to distinguish between the sanctions you use for rewarding *effort* and *responses.*
7. Have a general idea of the kinds of responses you are most likely to accept from children. *Caution:* do not reject good ideas simply because they do not fit your preconceived ideas. Reinforce correct ones and redirect incorrect or incomplete ones.

SUMMARY

In order to stimulate the student to higher cognitive thinking levels, the learner must be *actively* involved in the learning situation. Research shows the values of stimulating and guiding *student* questioning skills instead of always having teacher question-student answer. Practical suggestions are also presented for involving students in greater *pupil-to-pupil* interaction.

The importance is shown for increasing teacher wait-time between the question asking and the student answering. Practical suggestions are offered for teachers to use in evaluating and improving their uses of sanctions (rewards and punishments) in questioning.

4

HOW TO WRITE COGNITIVE DOMAIN QUESTIONS

Most psychologists believe that learning involves the interrelationship of cognitive (intellectual), affective (emotional), and psychomotor (manipulative) aspects. Benjamin Bloom and his associates have developed taxonomics for each of these learning domains. The learning model on page 54 shows the interrelationships between these domains. The separation, therefore, of the cognitive and affective domains in Bloom's books and this book is merely for closer analysis and discussion.

BLOOM'S COGNITIVE DOMAIN

The listing below presents Bloom's Cognitive Domain. The six divisions in this domain contain such intellectual behaviors as remembering, reasoning, problem solving, concept formation, and creative thinking. The taxonomy is constructed as a hierarchy, which means each division builds upon each preceding division. Therefore, the learner must have certain *Knowledge* (1.00) and *Comprehend* (2.00) the interrelationships of this knowledge before making an intelligent *Application* (3.00), etc. Cognitive development progresses from lower levels of inquiry (Knowledge 1.00) to the highest level (Evaluation 6.00).

Interrelationship Between Bloom's Domains[1]

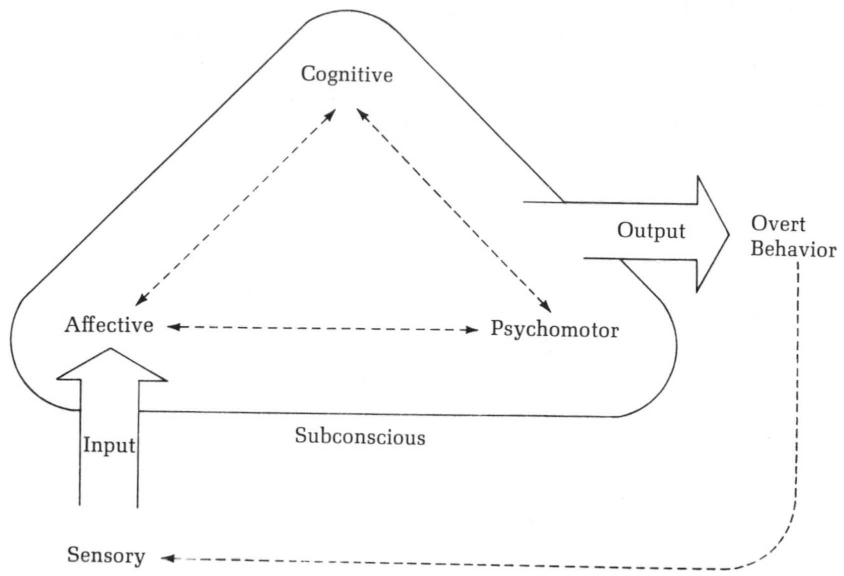

Bloom's Cognitive Domain[2]

1.00 KNOWLEDGE
- 1.10 Knowledge of specifics
  - 1.11 Knowledge of terminology
  - 1.12 Knowledge of specific facts
- 1.20 Knowledge of ways and means of dealing with specifics
  - 1.21 Knowledge of conventions
  - 1.22 Knowledge of trends and sequences
  - 1.23 Knowledge of classifications and categories
  - 1.24 Knowledge of criteria
  - 1.25 Knowledge of methodology
- 1.30 Knowledge of the universals and abstractions in a field
  - 1.31 Knowledge of principles and generalizations
  - 1.32 Knowledge of theories and structures

---

[1] A. F. Eiss and M. B. Harbeck, *Behavioral Objectives in the Affective Domain* (Washington, D.C.: National Science Teachers Association, 1969), p. 4.

[2] Adapted from Benjamin S. Bloom and David R. Krathwohl (eds.), *Taxonomy of Educational Objectives* (New York: David McKay Co., 1956) pp. 186–193. Used by permission of David McKay Company, Inc.

2.00 COMPREHENSION
- 2.10 Translation
- 2.20 Interpretation
- 2.30 Extrapolation

3.00 APPLICATION

4.00 ANALYSIS
- 4.10 Analysis of elements
- 4.20 Analysis of relationships
- 4.30 Analysis of organizational principles

5.00 SYNTHESIS
- 5.10 Production of a unique communication
- 5.20 Production of a plan, or proposed set of operations
- 5.30 Derivation of a set of abstract relations

6.00 EVALUATION
- 6.10 Judgments in terms of internal evidence
- 6.20 Judgments in terms of external criteria

Another way of viewing this progression is to observe the definitions of lower and higher levels of cognitive inquiry developed by a panel of judges in a research project and shown below:

Progression of Low to High Inquiry[3]

Low Inquiry: a learner based, cognitive process in which the student utilizes previously obtained knowledge in order to answer a question, posed by his teacher, which requires him to perform ONE of the following tasks:

1. provide or elicit the meaning of a term,
2. represent something by a word or phrase,
3. supply an example of something,
4. make statements of issues, steps in proofs, rules, conclusions, ideas, and beliefs that HAVE PREVIOUSLY BEEN MADE,

High Inquiry: a learner based, cognitive process in which the student utilizes previously obtained knowledge in order to answer a question, posed by his teacher, which required him to perform ONE of the following tasks:

1. perform an abstract operation, usually of a mathematical nature, such as multiplying, substitution, or simplifying,
2. rate some entity as to its value, dependability, importance, or sufficiency with a defense of the rating,

[3] George T. Ladd and Hans O. Andersen, "Determining the Level of Inquiry in Teacher's Questions," *Journal of Research in Science Teaching,* 7, (4), 1970, pp. 396–397.

Progression of Low to High Inquiry—(cont.)

5. supply a SUMMARY or a REVIEW of what was PREVIOUSLY SAID OR PROVIDED, or
6. place a given entity in the class to which it belongs UTILIZING CRITERIA ALREADY PROVIDED.

3. find similarities or differences in the qualities of two or more entities utilizing criteria defined BY THE STUDENT,
4. supply the consequent that is the result of some STATED condition, state, operation, object, or substance, or
5. provide evidence or reasoning to account for the occurrence of something (how or why it occurred).

WRITING COGNITIVE DOMAIN QUESTIONS

Questions are important teacher tools for guiding and evaluating the student's progress from one level of Bloom's Cognitive Domain to another. These questions may be asked to move the student's thinking to a higher cognitive level. In other situations, questions may be used to diagnose the student's cognitive level or to evaluate his progress. Both kinds of questions are presented now for Bloom's Cognitive Domain and for the Affective Domain in Chapter 5. Examples of questions from different subject fields are included for the major divisions of each domain.

1.00 Knowledge

The listing on page 54 shows the various levels of memory skills required in this cognitive division. Students are asked to recall materials to which they were previously exposed in classroom discussions, textbooks, films, etc. Some of the different kinds of knowledge and samples of a variety of ways of asking for recall are:

Terminology

Multiple Choice Question

What do we call money we pay for borrowing money?

1. insurance
2. premium
3. discount
4. interest

Matching Question

Match the correct statement *letter* with the corresponding principle *number* for each of these:

Statement	Principle
a. $a + b = b + a$	1. Associative law for addition
b. $(a \times b) \times c = a \times (b \times c)$	2. Associative law for multiplication
c. $a \times 0 = 0$	3. Commutative law for addition
d. $a \times b = b \times a$	4. Commutative law for multiplication
e. $a \times (b + c) = a \times b + a \times c$	5. Distributive law for multiplication
f. $a + (b + c) = (a + b) + c$	6. Identity element for addition
g. $a \times 1 = a \times \frac{2}{2} = \frac{2a}{2}$	7. Identity element for multiplication
h. $a + 0 = a$	8. Property of 0 in multiplication

Conventions

How would you pronounce the following commonly used food words in our language today as a result of our "cultural mix"?

1. pizza
2. blintzes
3. tacos
4. bagels
5. frijoles

Pictorial Question[4]

These pictures (top p. 58) show sugar cubes being ground.
Show the order in which they were taken.
Put numbers under the pictures.
What is your evidence?

[4] This order-of-events pictorial question is presented in Science Curriculum Improvement Study, *Material Objects Teacher's Guide* (New York: Rand McNally and Co., 1970), pp. 67; copyright by the Regents of the University of California, Berkeley, California 94720.

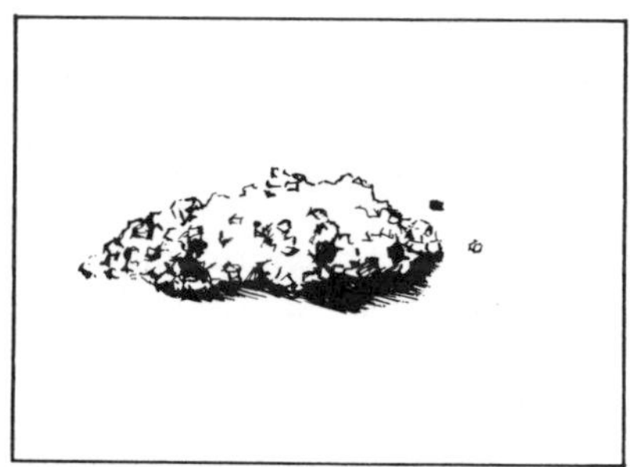

Classification and categories

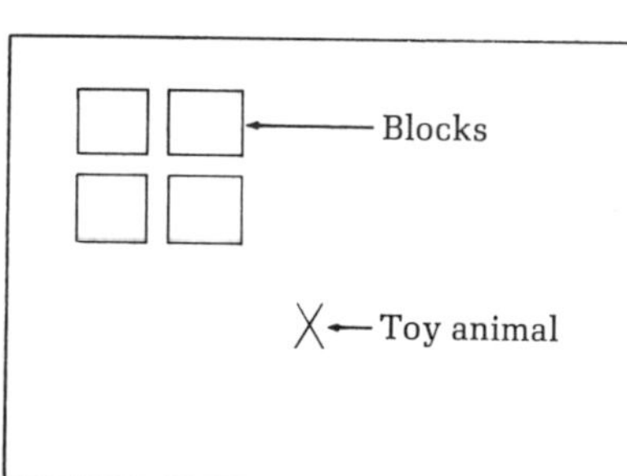

Field A Clustered Barns

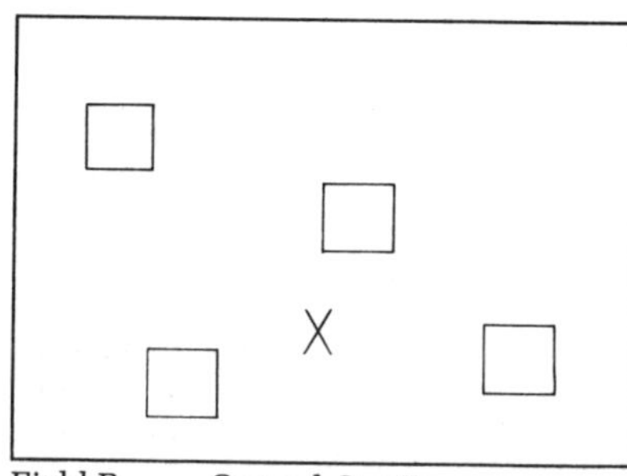
Field B Spread Out Barns

TASK 7.
Conservation of Area

Present the child with two identical pieces of green construction paper. Tell him these represent fields or pastures. Place one toy animal on each piece of paper.

Ask the child to compare the fields. Note they are the same size. Comment that since the fields are the same size each animal will have the same amount of grass to eat. Tell the child you are going to use blocks to represent barns.

Place four barns on each field as shown in Figure 7. (Leave the animal on the field.) Ask, "Now which animal will have the most grass to eat or will the amount of grass be the same?" **Justification**—"Why do you think this is true?" Continue adding equal numbers of barns to each field. Each time repeat the question, "Which animal will have the most grass to eat?"[5]

Knowledge of methodology
(techniques unique to a discipline of field of study)

"We have been studying statistics—the mathematics of chance and probability—and urban changes and population migrations for five weeks. What role(s) does statistics play in trying to understand and predict urban changes and population changes?"

Knowledge of Theories and Structures

"There is a theory that architecture is an adaptation of art found in the environment. Do you agree or disagree? Why?"

2.00 Comprehension

Questions in this division should be focused upon students developing skills in putting major ideas into their own thoughts and words, as well as seeing the relationships and applications of the major ideas.

Translation from one level of abstraction to another

"Sum up in one sentence what you think Sinclair Lewis was trying to say in *Martin Arrowsmith.*"

or

"Some young people say that they are "anti-establishment." However, they accept hand-outs from establishment people

[5] Rodger Bybee and Alan McCormack, "Applying Piaget's Theory," *Science and Children, 8* (4), December, 1970, p. 17. Reproduced with permission from *Science and Children,* December 1970. Copyright 1970 by the National Science Teachers Association, 1201 Sixteenth Street, N.W., Washington, D.C. 20036.

and justify this action by saying that society has an obligation to support them. This is an example of:

1. paranoid behavior
2. a "bad trip"
3. infantile thinking
4. rationalization
5. psychotic behavior

Translation from symbolic form to another form or vice versa

"The graphs on page 61[6] were produced in *Seventeen Magazine* to present visually the results of a survey of 2,000 young peoples (ages 14–22) opinions on current issues. Which of the graphs do *you* agree with most?"

or

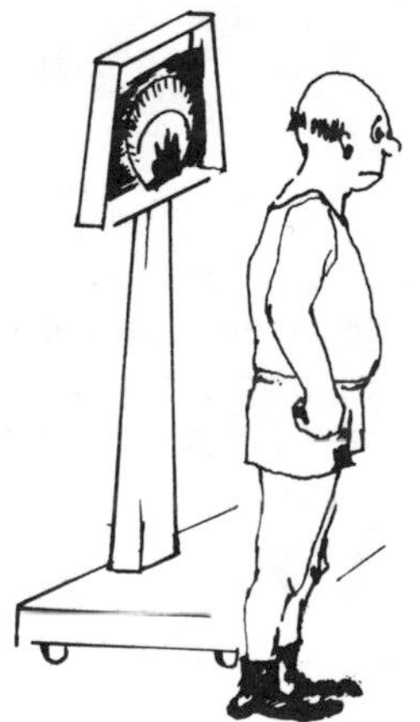

"According to the charts, George, you're going to have to lose some of that extra weight."

(Questions follow on page 62.)

[6] "You Tell What's Right & Wrong With America," reprinted from *Seventeen*® Vol. 30, No. 2, February, 1971, pp. 116–127. Copyright © 1971 by Triangle Publications, Inc.

How Young People Feel the Government Spends Our Money

POLLUTION CONTROL

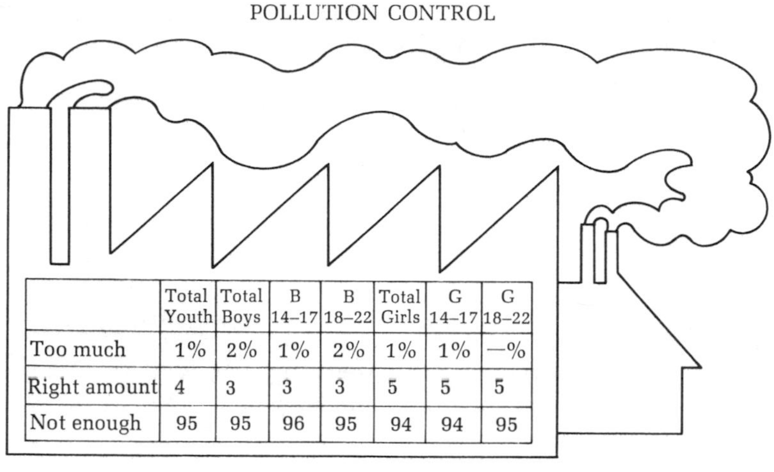

	Total Youth	Total Boys	B 14–17	B 18–22	Total Girls	G 14–17	G 18–22
Too much	1%	2%	1%	2%	1%	1%	—%
Right amount	4	3	3	3	5	5	5
Not enough	95	95	96	95	94	94	95

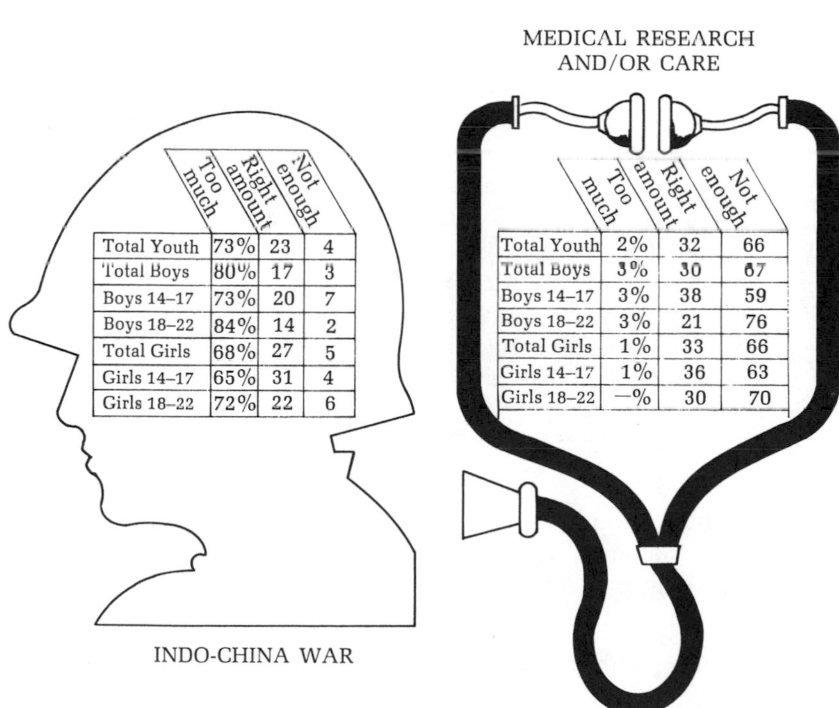

MEDICAL RESEARCH AND/OR CARE

	Too much	Right amount	Not enough
Total Youth	2%	32	66
Total Boys	3%	30	67
Boys 14–17	3%	38	59
Boys 18–22	3%	21	76
Total Girls	1%	33	66
Girls 14–17	1%	36	63
Girls 18–22	—%	30	70

INDO-CHINA WAR

	Too much	Right amount	Not enough
Total Youth	73%	23	4
Total Boys	80%	17	3
Boys 14–17	73%	20	7
Boys 18–22	84%	14	2
Total Girls	68%	27	5
Girls 14–17	65%	31	4
Girls 18–22	72%	22	6

The cartoon on page 60 illustrates that:

1. People in the United States have greater obesity problems than anywhere else in the world.
2. The doctor doesn't practice what he preaches.
3. The doctor was being facetious.
4. The patient hasn't been watching weight charts closely enough.
5. None of the above.
6. All of 1-4.

Interpretation (sees relationships between major ideas)

"Using the information presented in the previous graphs (on page 61), select the category from A to E that is best for statements in 1–5."

1. Girls 18–22 feel government spends too much for pollution control.
2. Boys 14–17 don't care what government spends on medical research and/or care.
3. Girls are more interested in being nurses than boys.
4. Boys 18–22 do not want to fight in the Indo-China War.
5. 95% of all youth questioned felt the government did not spend enough for pollution control.

A. *definitely* true
B. *probably* true
C. insufficient data to make choice
D. *probably* false
E. *definitely* false

or

"Compare the plans of Martin Luther King, Booker T. Washington, Malcolm X, and Huey Newton to promote the interests of Blacks in America."

Extrapolation (can go beyond data to implications of major ideas)

"Each year the government publishes the ratios of employed to unemployed workers. Why is such data inadequate for determining the employment status of migrant workers, autoworkers, lifeguards, and lumbermen?"

or

"Population migration tends to be in the direction of urban areas and away from rural areas. There is also a tendency for minority members to locate in slum areas near central business districts of large cities. Why do you think this is so?"

3.00 Application

Students use previously acquired *Knowledge* and *Comprehension* to solve problems in new or unique situations.

"Now that we have studied heat for some time, see if you can apply your understandings to these new situations:

1. According to your understanding of ENERGY SOURCE-ENERGY SINK, why is this common statement inaccurate:

   Close the door, you're letting in the cold!
2. How would you correct the above statement to make it accurate?
3. Using the above knowledge, how could you account for getting a bad *burn* if you touch dry ice?"

or

Each child is assigned or volunteers to be one of the countries in the United Nations. They role-play the operations of the U.N.'s General Assembly after being assigned to:

1. Become familiar with the operations and issues of the General Assembly.
2. Select an agenda of topical issues.
3. Research the nations they will represent and how they have reacted in the past to issues.
4. Prepare what they anticipate to be "their nation's" stand on the issues.

4.00 Analysis

Students are asked to reduce ideas into their component parts and to show that they understand the relationship of the parts.

The difference between this category and interpretation and application is:

Interpretation and application—emphasis upon using subject matter to arrive at conclusions.

Analysis—concern also for subject matter but learner must be conscious of the intellectual process he is performing and know the rules for reaching valid conclusions.

The subdivisions of *analysis* gives some clues to the specifics of reasoning being sought:

4:10–Analysis of Elements
4:20–Analysis of Relationships
4:30–Analysis of Organizational Principles

Analysis of elements (break down into parts and show relationship)

In this cartoon activity[7] the learner is asked to separate observations from inferences:

Activity 1

Give each child a set of cartoons . . . and ask the children to look at Cartoon 1. Tell them about the two boys: **Andrew, the taller boy, is seven years old. He naturally thinks he knows much more than Mike, who is only five years old. Mike always has his own opinion, however, and he puts up an argument.**

Tell the children to read the cartoon story to find out why Andrew and Mike are arguing. After they have read the story, begin a discussion of the frames by asking questions and inferences. Here are some examples:

What was the disagreement about? (How the bike got wet. Andrew said that it must have rained. Mike said that maybe his mother had watered the lawn.)

Why did Andrew infer that it had rained? (He observed that the ground and the tricycle were wet.)

Did Andrew see the rain? (No.)

Why did Mike infer that Mother had watered the lawn? (From the same observation—that the ground was wet.)

---

[7] *Science—A Process Approach,* Exercise A, Part D, Revised Ed. American Association for the Advancement of Science/Xerox Corporation, 1968. Reprinted by permission.

Did Mike see his mother water the lawn? (No.)

What made Andrew think that it had rained? (He knows from past experience that rain makes the ground wet.)

Could Mike be right when he says that his mother watered the lawn? (Yes.)

How many children think that Andrew is right?

Why

How many think that both are right?
Why?
Can we decide which boy is right? (No.)
Why not?
Should we make further observations? (Yes.) **Why?** (We do not have enough information yet.)

After some class discussion, have the children complete their copies of the question sheet given below:

Questions for Cartoon 1

Which of the following statements are observations? Which are inferences? Circle *O* if you think the statement is an *observation;* circle *I* if you think it is an *inference.*

The ground is wet.	(O)	I
The tricycle has water drops on it.	(O)	I
It rained while we were sleeping.	O	(I)
Mother watered the lawn.	O	(I)

Which senses did Andrew and Mike use to make the observations? (Sight.)

What would you do to find out which boy is right in the inference he made? (Try to get more information. For example, we might examine the yard next door, or see if the hose is wet, or ask Mother.)

(*Note:* The suggestions in parentheses here and the answers circled above are for you and are not on the question sheet.)

Analysis of relationships

The following exercise[8] attempts to develop students perceptions of cause-effect relationships:

Tell whether each of the statements following the fact is:

A. A cause of the fact
B. A result of the fact
C. Not related to the fact

Fact: A flash of lightning occurs.

Statements

3. A roar of thunder can be heard. 3. ______
4. Electricity passed between clouds and the earth. 4. ______
5. It is dangerous to stand under a tree during a rainstorm 5. ______

---

[8] Nelson B. Henry (ed.), "The Measurement of Understanding," *The Forty-fifth Yearbook of the National Society for the Study of Education, Part I* (Chicago: University of Chicago Press, 1946), p. 135.

Fact: Metals expand when heated.

Statements

12. The molecules of metal become farther apart when heated. 12. ______
13. When the temperature increases, the mercury in the thermometer rises. 13. ______
14. Telephone wires are slack in summer and tighter in winter. 14. ______

Analysis of organizational principles

Students are asked to show that they can reconstruct the processes by which the ideas were formulated. An example of this questioning is:

"Analyze what you consider to be the reasoning that may have gone on in the minds of the people who made these statements:

1. Students who engage in 'Anti-establishment' causes are frustrated, sick kids.
2. The Black Panthers should be disbanded and arrested because they preach race hatred and segregation.
3. America is the greatest country in the world because our gross national income is the highest of any nation in history.
4. The Democratic Party is a party of war-mongers because it was in power during World War II."

5.00 Synthesis

Unlike analysis (which breaks a whole into its parts), synthesis asks students to put parts together to made patterns that are new to *them.* This requires much higher creative thinking processes, which Bloom has divided into three subcategories:

5:10–Production of a Unique Communication
5:20–Production of a Plan or Proposed Set of Operations
5:30–Derivation of a Set of Abstract Relations

The stress in these subcategories is upon *divergent thinking.* That is, a problem is presented in an open-ended fashion and *as many solutions as possible* are encouraged. Reference to the student's life situation is seen as desirable in selecting sources of problems for study.

Production of a unique communication

For younger children, the teacher might structure this type of question:

"We have just come back from our trip to our city's water purification plant. For homework tonight, write your answers to these questions so that we can discuss them tomorrow."

1. I agree with the Water Commissioner that big industries in our town are polluting our waters because . . .
2. I disagree with the Water Commissioner that little can be done to correct the pollution because . . .

Older students could address themselves to such local situations as:

1. High school students should have a say in deciding dress rule regulations because . . .
2. A request to build an atomic power plant outside the city should *not* be granted because . . .
3. Girls should be drafted along with men because . . .

Production of a plan or proposed set of operations

Here we ask student to move from "cookbook experiences" where everything is planned out for him. He is asked to devise other ways of investigating by such questions as:

"We just finished studying about static electricity and ways of producing and controlling it. Use that information to answer:

"Why do you get a 'shock' everytime you slide across the plastic seat covers in your father's car? How would you devise ways to prevent the shock?"

or

Devise a plan to study whether students who go to church every week are better citizens than those who do not.

Derivation of a set of abstract relations

Students are encouraged to formulate hypotheses to explain elements of phenomena they analyze. To do so, they might first be helped to learn how to ask the "right" questions with such exercises as:

> "We are on a class picnic and field day. As the bus stops at the park, three students volunteer to find a good picnic spot for us. They all come back excited about their finds for the best spot. What questions would you ask to decide which spot to pick?"

After students develop skill at questioning-asking, experience could be gotten in formulating hypothesis:

1. How many hypotheses do you have for the Scandanavian countries having one of the world's highest suicide rates?
2. Can you propose a hypothesis that would explain why Republican Ronald Reagan won in California in 1969 even though the state overwhelmingly elected a Democratic senator?

Another aspect of this subcategory would ask students to consider alternate courses of action such as:

1. If John Fitzgerald Kennedy had not been assassinated, what possible course of action might he have pursued with respect to Vietnam?
2. What are some of the possible things the Parent-Teachers-Student Association might do to inform the community of the need for an addition to our high school?

Eventually, the student should be assisted in planning and carrying out (wherever possible) appropriate action. This is not only an application activity, but involves higher creative thinking. You might suggest that students:

1. Select a current local issue before the state legislature to which students are committed and one that *directly* affects their lives. They could contact their legislative representative and jointly devise a plan that class could follow to work for the bill to be passed.
2. Select a current school issue and plan to work for the solution they support.

6:00 Evaluation

Evaluation, the most complex of all learning, is the blending of knowledge, comprehension, application, analysis, and synthesis. Students are required to perform two steps in evaluation:

6:10–*Judgements in Terms of Internal Evidence* (set up appropriate standards or values).
6:20–*Judgements in Terms of External Criteria* (determine how closely the idea or objects meets these standards or values).

Although the next chapter goes into great detail on the role of values in Bloom's Affective Domain, some mention should be made here of values of evaluation. The student should be helped to distinguish between fact and values by questions such as those which follow.

Judgments in terms of internal evidence

"Which of the following are statements of fact and which are statements of values?"

1. Washington, D.C. is located on the Potomac River.
2. A capital city should be located near the center of the nation.
3. Philadelphia was our national capital before Washington, D.C.
4. That government is best which governs least.

The above type of exercise reveals that the dividing line between fact and value is not always clear or easy to identify. All values are opinions in the sense that values cannot be proven to be true or false. However, all opinions are not values, because opinions often result from lack of access to information or may take the form of predictions. This understanding can be developed by such a question as:

"Indicate whether each of the following is a 'fact,' 'value,' or an 'opinion that is not of value'."

1. Wars are bad.
2. The United States participated in two world wars in the first half of the twentieth century.

3. Neither the United States nor Russia will start a nuclear war, because the leaders of both realize that it would mean mutual destruction.
4. I'm willing to wager that if you check the record you will find that the federal debt increased every year, except one, of the Eisenhower administration.
5. Economic freedom is the most important need of the American farmer.

or

"Describe the fallacies in reasoning in this statement:

All Ducks are birds.
All Robins are birds.
Therefore, all ducks are robins."

Judgments in terms of external criteria

A practical example of how well the idea meets the standards or values established to judge it could be this situation:

The class established the following list of characteristics that their families considered before they moved into our community:

1. Access to different kinds of transportation (trains, buses, automobile routes, etc.).
2. Low property tax rate
3. Good schools
4. Houses of worship
5. Availability of "cultural activities"
6. Similar ages of children in neighborhood
7. Availability and adequacy of moderately priced services such as garbage collection, etc.

---

1. To what extent does our community meet these considerations?
2. What sources did you use to make your judgement in No. 1 above?
3. Are there additional considerations to be included now that you've lived in the community for awhile?

SUMMARY

The six intellectual divisions and their interrelationship of Bloom's Cognitive Domain were presented. Definitions of and questions for each of these divisions were given:

1.00 Knowledge
2.00 Comprehension
3.00 Application
4.00 Analysis
5.00 Synthesis
6.00 Evaluation

5

HOW TO WRITE QUESTIONS FOR THE AFFECTIVE DOMAIN

The *Cognitive* Domain deals with knowledge and intellectual understanding. The *Affective* Domain deals with emotion, interests, attitudes, values, and appreciations. This latter suggests the influence of the student's feelings upon how he is *affected* by his learning, as well as how his feelings *affect* his learning.

RELATIONSHIP BETWEEN COGNITIVE AND AFFECTIVE DOMAIN

It is apparent that both the cognitive and affective domains are involved in what we call thinking, learning, and behaving. The illustration on page 54 in Chapter 4 presents a learning model showing the interrelationships between the domains. Eiss and Harbeck point out the vital role the affective domain plays in the learning process in that model in this way:

> The affective domain is central to every part of the learning and evaluation process. It begins with the threshold of consciousness, where awareness of the stimulus initiates the learning process. It provides the threshold for evaluation, where willingness to respond is the basis for psychomotor responses, without which no evaluation of the learning process can take place. It includes values and value systems that provide the basis for continued learning and for most of an individual's overt behaviors. It provides the bridge between the

stimulus and the cognitive and the psychomotor aspects of an individual's personality.[1]

Krathwohl and his associates also stress the close relationships between the affective and cognitive domains. It is fully recognized by them that any division of domains is arbitrary. They list these five broad categories of educational objectives in the affective domain:

Receiving
Responding
Valuing
Organization of Values
Characterization of a Value or Value Complex

The chart below shows the overlap of the affective and cognitive domains. The italicized names are the domain heads and their corresponding numbers are in the parentheses. By combining the ideas in the illustration on page 54 in Chapter 4 and this chart, some of these relationships between the domains can be readily seen.

Relations Between the Cognitive and Affective Domains[2]

Cognitive Domain	*Affective Domain*
1. The cognitive continuum begins with the student's recall and recognition of *Knowledge* (1.0).	1. The affective continuum begins with the student's merely *Receiving* (1.0) stimuli and
2. it extends through his *Comprehension* (2.0) of the knowledge.	2. his *Responding* (2.0) to stimuli on request, willingly responding to these stimuli, and taking satisfaction in this responding.
3. his skill in *Application* (3.0) of the knowledge that he comprehends.	3. his *Valuing* (3.0) the phenomenon or activity so that he voluntarily responds and seeks out ways to respond.

[1] Albert F. Eiss and Mary Blatt Harbeck, *Behavioral Objectives in the Affective Domain* (Washington, D.C.: National Science Teachers Association, 1969), p. 11.

[2] David R. Krathwohl, Benjamin S. Bloom, and Bertram B. Masia, *Taxonomy of Educational Objectives*, Handbook II: Affective Domain (New York: David McKay Co., Inc., 1964), pp. 49–50. Used by permission of David McKay Company, Inc.

Cognitive Domain	*Affective Domain*
4. his skill in *Analysis* (4.0) of situations involving this knowledge, his skill in *Synthesis* (5.0) of this knowledge into new organizations.	4. his *Conceptualization* (4.1) of each value responded to.
5. his skill in *Evaluation* (6.0) in that area of knowledge to judge the value of material and methods for given purposes.	5. his *Organization* (4.2) of these values into systems and finally organizing the value complex into a single whole, a *Characterization* (5.0) of the individual.

Difficulties in Developing and Assessing Affective Domain Objectives

Most psychologists and teachers recognize the importance and interrelationship of the affective domain in learning. However, developing and evaluating objectives in the affective domain have not proceeded at the rate that the cognitive domain has because:

Deterrents to Affective Domain Development

Private-Public Status of Cognitive and Affective Domains	1. Achievement and competence in cognitive areas are regarded as *public* matters in our Judeo-Christian culture (dean's list, publishing of scholarship winners by newspapers, etc.) In contrast, however, one's personality traits, attitudes, values, and beliefs are regarded as *private* matters (religious and political beliefs, etc.).
Home and Church vs. Public Schools	2. Following closely upon #1 above, is the historical place of and belief in the teaching of affective domain taking place in the home and church and not in the schools.
Emphasis Upon Cognitive Learning	3. The pressure to keep the affective domain out of the schools has resulted in the greatest emphasis and time commitment of the public schools being placed on the cognitive of education.

Deterrents to Affective Domain Development—(cont.)

Teacher Expectations	4. A corollary to #3 is the feeling of comfort that teachers have when they teach facts, principles, and generalizations. Possibly, this is due to the ways in which teachers themselves were taught and partly perhaps because they think it is the way the public expects them to teach.
Education vs. Indoctrination	5. *Education* is seen by many as an almost cognitive examination of issues. *Indoctrination,* on the other hand, has come to mean the teaching of affective as well as cognitive aspects of learning.
Cognitive—Immediate: Affective—Long Time	6. Cognitive aspects of learning are relatively quickly acquired and can be immediately tested. In contrast, personality characteristics, attitudes, and interests are presumed to take place relatively slowly and tested only over a long period of time.
Easier to Measure Cognitive Domain	7. It is easier to evaluate the outcomes of cognitive goals than it is to measure outcomes of affective goals. One reason may be that cognitive goals have been more clearly defined. Also, adequate measures of affective domain are hard to find and schools generally teach that which can be tested.

In spite of the above reasons, there is a definite trend toward the inclusion of the affective domain in the objectives and evaluation of teaching and learning. The reasons for the increased interest in the affective domain have been summarized by William Carr in his discussion of the selection of the title for the Fourth International Curriculum Conference in 1969:

> "*Values and the curriculum*" is an important theme not merely because of its long-range considerations, but also because, at this particular point in history, the growth of science and technology, the declining influence of organized religion, the in-

creased emphasis upon material goods, and the alienation of many young people are among the factors which combine to make this theme not only significant but urgent.[3]

AFFECTIVE DOMAIN STRUCTURE

Krathwohl, Bloom, and Masia developed these category and subcategory titles for their Affective Domain:[4]

- 1.0 Receiving (attending)
  - 1.1 Awareness
  - 1.2 Willingness to receive
  - 1.3 Controlled or selected attention
- 2.0 Responding
  - 2.1 Acquiescence in responding
  - 2.2 Willingness to respond
  - 2.3 Satisfaction in response
- 3.0 Valuing
  - 3.1 Acceptance of a value
  - 3.2 Preference for a value
  - 3.3 Commitment (conviction)
- 4.0 Organization
  - 4.1 Conceptualization of a value
  - 4.2 Organization of a value system
- 5.0 Characterization by a value or value complex
  - 5.1 Generalized set
  - 5.2 Characterization

If teachers are to effectively use the affective domain, it is important that they concentrate on these objectives with greater effort than has been the case traditionally. Krathwohl has taken commonly-used, broad educational terms and objectives such as interest, attitude, appreciation, value clarification, and adjustment and correlated these to affective domain categories and subcategories as indicated in the chart on page 78.

To assist teachers who wish to include affective domain objectives in their teaching, each category and subcategory will

[3] William G. Carr (ed.), *Values and the Curriculum. A Report of the Fourth International Curriculum Conference* (Washington, D.C.: National Education Association, 1970), pp. 5–6.

[4] Krathwohl, et al., p. 35.

The Range of Meaning Typical of Commonly Used Affective Terms Measured against the Taxonomy Continuum.[5]

5.0 Characterization by a Value Complex		4.0 Organization		3.0 Valuing			2.0 Responding			1.0 Receiving		
5.2	5.1	4.2	4.1	3.3	3.2	3.1	2.3	2.2	2.1	1.3	1.2	1.1
Characterization	Generalized set	Organization of a value system	Conceptualization of a value	Commitment	Preference for a value	Acceptance of a value	Satisfaction in response	Willingness to respond	Acquiescence in responding	Controlled or selected attention	Willingness to receive	Awareness

Adjustment

Value

Attitudes

Appreciation

Interest

[5] Ibid., p. 37.

now be expanded to include definitions, suggestions for writing questions for each category, and other appropriate teaching techniques.

1.0 Receiving (attending)

The teacher is interested in developing and assessing sensitivity in the learner to certain stimuli and phenomena. For instance, on one of the simpler levels, it could be the teacher helping the learner become aware of different hues and color saturations. This relatively simple affective level is needed by the learner if he is to develop higher levels of awareness. And, of course, awareness is necessary before *any* learning takes place. However, what the learner brings to the classroom situation from previous formal and informal experiences may facilitate or hinder his sensitivity to what the teacher is trying to teach him. One of the authors of this text found that even simple teaching acts intended by the teachers to be positive and helpful to learners may be seen as threatening, hostile, and negative. This predetermined perception occurred because of previous experiences and self-concepts learners bring to the classroom.[6]

Receiving has three subcategories showing the full range of attending to stimuli from the extreme passive role of a learner to a point at which the learner is able to direct his attention toward a preferred stimuli:

1.1 Awareness
1.2 Willingness to Receive
1.3 Controlled or Selected Attention

The gradations of the three subcategories are slight and difficult to separate. The major difference is the *degree of consciousness* of a stimuli or phenomena. The following kinds of questioning situations might be presented for developing and assessing progress in each of the subcategories.

---

[6] Arthur A. Carin, "Children's Perceptions of Selected Teaching Acts" (Unpublished doctoral dissertation, Salt Lake City, Utah: University of Utah, 1958).

Note: Jean Piaget sees intelligence as the building of experiences on each other, forming ever more complex structures or schemas. *Sensory* experiences are vital in Piaget's view of development. For further information see Carole Honstead, "The Developmental Theory of Jean Piaget" in Joe L. Frost (Ed.), *Early Childhood Education Rediscovered* (New York: Holt, Rinehart & Winston, Inc. 1968), pp. 132–145.

1.1 Awareness (merely conscious of a situation, person, phenomenon, object or state of affairs)

Often, a person may not be able to verbalize why he is aware of a particular phenomenon. Teachers, especially in social studies, assist learners with developing awareness of the existence of statesmen in national and international affairs. Such an activity, on this level of awareness, might take this form:

"Please fill in the missing blanks for either the statesman or country. Refer to reference books if needed."

Statesman	*Country*
Pierre Trudeau	____________
Fidel Castro	____________
____________	South Vietnam
Catherine Devlin	____________
Chiang Kai Chek	____________
____________	Great Britain
____________	Egypt

Another technique useful in making inferences of students' awareness is the *free-association* activity about people in the news. Student responses can be examined in terms of both the existence of awareness as well as the depth of it. The teacher could say:

"Please write *any* word, phrase, or sentence which each of the following names of people suggests. Cover all names below the one you are working on and answer as quickly as possible."

Richard Nixon ________________________
Joe Namath ________________________
Robert Kennedy ________________________
Charles DeGaulle ________________________
Ronald Reagan ________________________
The Beatles ________________________
Lyndon B. Johnson ________________________

"Now that you have written about these people, look back over your words. Why did you select the words you did? Would you change any? How? Why?"

1.2 Willingness to receive

Although this subcategory is at a higher level of awareness, the learner is not *actively* seeking out stimuli. At best, the learner is willing to notice the stimulus and give it his attention. He does not actively *avoid* the phenomenon. Questioning in this subcategory centers around the negative rather than the positive. By this, we mean that we are looking for the absence of a rejection of the stimulus. The learner is said to have a tolerance for the stimulus rather than finding it attractive or being drawn to it.

An *interest-inventory* can be used for appraisal of the Willingness to Receive subcategory. The teacher may vary the subject matter and change the questions and situations. The following interest inventory could be given to students after they return from an assigned visit to an Art Museum:

> "You have spent several hours at the Art Museum. Please respond to the following questions concerning your feelings about your visit. Circle the letter of the answer which best describes your feelings."

Question	*Select One*
1. How interesting was your visit?	a. very interesting b. somewhat interesting c. not too interesting d. not at all interesting
2. Which art form held your attention best?	a. sculpture b. paintings c. wood carvings d. block printing
3. How do you feel about the amount of time that should have been spent in the museum?	a. less b. same c. more d. much more
4. Are there any art pieces you would like to see again some time soon?	a. yes b. no
5. Which period of art interested you most?	a. Contemporary b. Renaissance c. Ming Dynasty

English teachers, interested especially in general semantics, could also work on this category. They could give the following kind of assignment to help students become aware of language and its differing levels.

"Describe yourself as if you were:

Your father
Your mother
Your sister or brother
Your best friend
Your favorite teacher
The teacher you like least
Someone else's father or mother
Your barber

In what ways do these descriptions differ? Why do you think they are different?"

1.3 Controlled or selected attention

The learner is able to focus or control his attention. *Forced-choice* interest inventories enable teachers to examine selectively students' patterns of preferences which can then be shown to the student. The following two forced-choice interest inventories are suggestive of an almost endless variety for any and all testing of areas of selected attention.

"Please respond to the following questions by placing the letter in the blank space that best expresses your feelings."

If the following TV programs came on, I would respond by:

A. Watching it with much enjoyment
B. Watching it but enjoying it little
C. Changing to another program

1. Westerns________________
2. News broadcasts____________
3. Cartoons ________________
4. Musicals ________________
5. Talk Shows ______________
6. Sports Games _____________
7. Quiz Shows ______________
8. Situation Comedies__________

9. Religious ____________
10. Political Debates ____________
11. Others (Specify) ____________

This forced choice test attempts to examine the learner's attention of science support statements as well as his opinions of them:

Inventory—Science Support Scale[7]

We would like to know your opinions regarding the following 58 statements about science and scientists. Please indicate the extent of your agreement or disagreement with each statement by circling the appropriate number at the right of each statement.

5 – I STRONGLY AGREE with the statement.
4 – I AGREE with the statement.
3 – I am UNDECIDED about the statement.
2 – I DISAGREE with the statement.
1 – I STRONGLY DISAGREE with the statement.

	SA	A	U	D	SD
1. One important function of science is to demonstrate the wonder and orderliness of God's universe.	5	4	3	2	1
2. It is likely that much of the scientific information we have today will be demonstrated to be inaccurate or inadequate in the future.	5	4	3	2	1
3. If one or two scientists have evidence which appears to contradict current scientific belief, they are probably wrong.	5	4	3	2	1
4. Science would be better off if scientists of Communist and non-Communist countries could work together.	5	4	3	2	1
5. Religious leaders should be constantly on guard against the ideas and theories that scientists produce and explore.	5	4	3	2	1

[7] Patricia M. Schwirian, "Construction and Validation of a Science Support Scale," Doctoral Dissertation, the Ohio State University, 1967.

Item	SA	A	U	D	SD
6. Science is bound to lead our society into godlessness.	5	4	3	2	1
7. The skepticism of the scientist should be limited to his work.	5	4	3	2	1
53. All miracles have a scientific explanation.	5	4	3	2	1
54. Scientists go overboard on demanding evidence before drawing conclusions.	5	4	3	2	1
55. It will be a good thing when machines free men of all manual labor.	5	4	3	2	1
56. When doing medical research, scientists should be able to collect information of a highly personal nature.	5	4	3	2	1
57. More federal support to science should be in the form of grants for general scholarship and exploratory research rather than contracts for specified product research.	5	4	3	2	1
58. In the long run, man's lot will be improved by scientific knowledge.	5	4	3	2	1

2.0 Responding

Up to this point, the learner has been involved with being aware of and attending to stimuli. Now, the learner is doing something with or about the stimuli, not merely perceiving it. The three subcategories of this class, Responding, are:

Subcategory	*Basic Affective Element*
2.1 Acquiescence in responding	Compliance—passiveness
2.2 Willingness to respond	More responsibility for initiating action
2.3 Satisfaction in response	Emotional response of pleasure, zest or enjoyment

2.1 Acquiescence in responding

At the first level of this class, the learner *actively* responds. There is more the element of compliance than real zealousness. If there were real free choice, the student might take an action other than acquiescence. Although teachers strive to reduce acquiescence and to stimulate *student initiation* of action, the basic question in this subcategory is:

> Does the student actually respond in a way that can be observed directly or determined by asking the student?

One way to assess whether the student responses are self-initiated or mere compliance is to devise a *parent questionnaire*. The following example of such a questionnaire examines the student's behavior in relation to following traffic rules outside of school.

Dear Parent:

Our class has been investigating pedestrian and vehicular traffic regulations, how they originated, possible reasons for their modifications when needed, and what effect, if any, they have on the prevention or reduction of pedestrian and vehicular accidents.

I am conducting a survey to see if our school traffic program has had any carry-over into your child's traffic behavior outside of school. To assist me, could you please spend a few minutes and complete the enclosed form concerning your observation of ____________'s out-of-school traffic behavior? Please put a check on the line at the point that shows only behavior you have *observed*. Please send the completed form to me in the enclosed self-addressed envelope. No one will see this form besides me. Thank you for your cooperation.

Respectfully,
(signed)
Miss Orkand

Directions

Please place a checkmark any place along the line where your child is functioning according to what you have personally observed. Please note the category "Insufficient Observations," should you feel that you do not know how your child functions in that area.

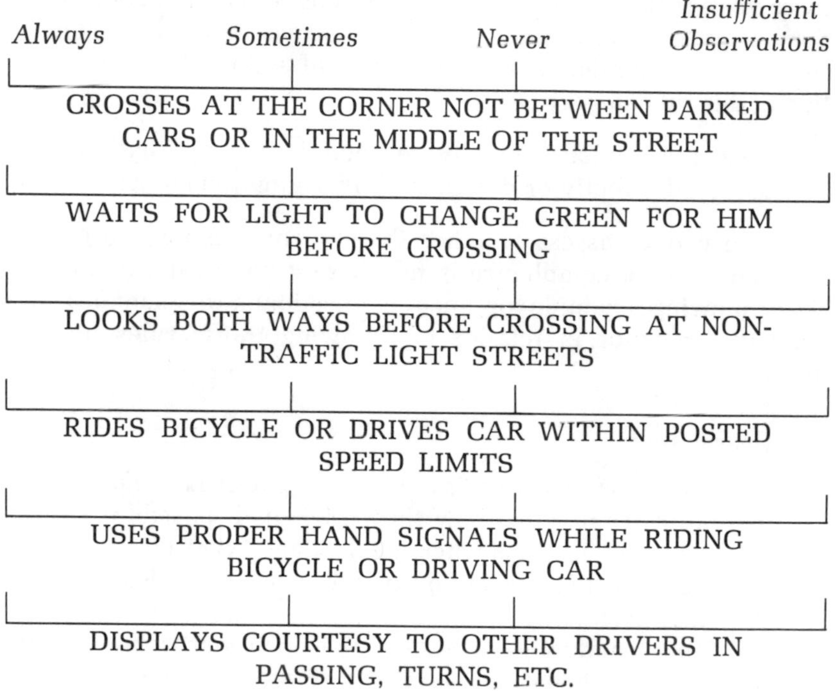

Always | *Sometimes* | *Never* | *Insufficient Observations*

CROSSES AT THE CORNER NOT BETWEEN PARKED CARS OR IN THE MIDDLE OF THE STREET

WAITS FOR LIGHT TO CHANGE GREEN FOR HIM BEFORE CROSSING

LOOKS BOTH WAYS BEFORE CROSSING AT NON-TRAFFIC LIGHT STREETS

RIDES BICYCLE OR DRIVES CAR WITHIN POSTED SPEED LIMITS

USES PROPER HAND SIGNALS WHILE RIDING BICYCLE OR DRIVING CAR

DISPLAYS COURTESY TO OTHER DRIVERS IN PASSING, TURNS, ETC.

Another useful instrument in this subcategory is the story-*situation projective device*. A situation is presented in which an activity involves the behavior the teacher wishes to evaluate. An open-ended question follows the story description so that the student may project how he thinks the situation will end. Below is an example of an open-ended story situation[8] depicting students' reactions to library or school book regulations. The respondents' answers reveal much about their degree of acquiescence to regulations.

---

[8] Arthur A. Carin and Marie Hughes, *School Situation Perception Test.* All rights reserved. Further information may be obtained from Arthur A. Carin, Queens College of the City University of New York, Flushing, New York 11367.

Charlie came to the teacher with a health book:

Charlie: Miss Smith, may I borrow this book overnight, so I can finish my work?

Teacher: Yes—but you bring it to me first thing in the morning, so I'll know you brought it back.

Question: How would you feel if you were Charlie?

Question: Would you bring the book back the next day?

2.2 *Willingness to respond*

The teacher must devise appraisal situations to directly or indirectly observe students' willing initiation of action. It is not necessary to delve into the motivation for the student responding willingly, but sufficient for the student to make a selection and act. Below is an example of alternative actions students could select during their Christmas vacation.

An Open-Ended List of Alternatives for a Christmas Vacation[9]

Directions: Below are some activities various people were involved in during Christmas vacation. We need some other ideas from *you.* When the list is long enough, we would like to ask each of you to categorize the items in the following ways:

X–This is definitely not for me.
U–Unlikely that I would do it.
N–Neutral or unsure.
P–Possibly I would do this in the future.
A–I affirm this; I will definitely try to build it into my life, if I have not already done so.

_______ 1. Worked up a show and performed it in a hospital ward.
_______ 2. Made up a basket of food and delivered it to some needy family
_______ 3. Organized a group to go caroling in the neighborhood.
_______ 4. Invited some children from an underprivileged neighborhood to spend a day with me and returned the visit.

[9] Louis E. Raths, Merrill Harmin, and Sidney B. Simon, *Values and Teaching* (Columbus, Ohio: Charles E. Merrill Publishing Co., 1966), pp. 243–245.

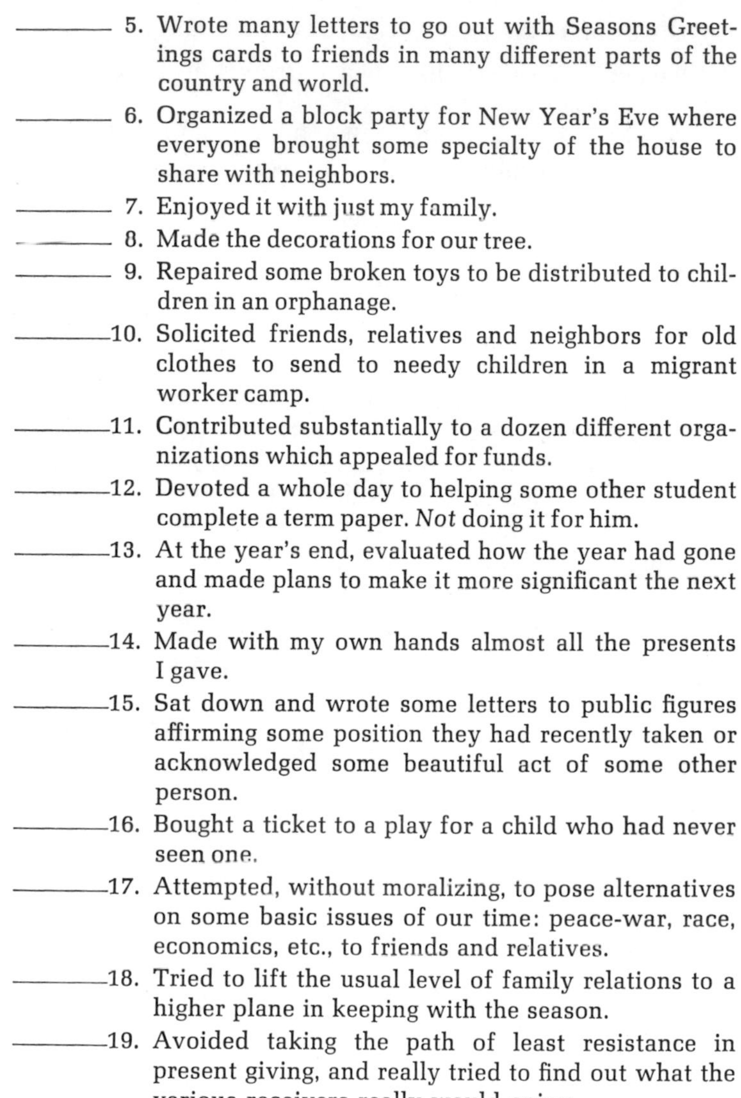

________ 5. Wrote many letters to go out with Seasons Greetings cards to friends in many different parts of the country and world.

________ 6. Organized a block party for New Year's Eve where everyone brought some specialty of the house to share with neighbors.

________ 7. Enjoyed it with just my family.

________ 8. Made the decorations for our tree.

________ 9. Repaired some broken toys to be distributed to children in an orphanage.

________10. Solicited friends, relatives and neighbors for old clothes to send to needy children in a migrant worker camp.

________11. Contributed substantially to a dozen different organizations which appealed for funds.

________12. Devoted a whole day to helping some other student complete a term paper. *Not* doing it for him.

________13. At the year's end, evaluated how the year had gone and made plans to make it more significant the next year.

________14. Made with my own hands almost all the presents I gave.

________15. Sat down and wrote some letters to public figures affirming some position they had recently taken or acknowledged some beautiful act of some other person.

________16. Bought a ticket to a play for a child who had never seen one.

________17. Attempted, without moralizing, to pose alternatives on some basic issues of our time: peace-war, race, economics, etc., to friends and relatives.

________18. Tried to lift the usual level of family relations to a higher plane in keeping with the season.

________19. Avoided taking the path of least resistance in present giving, and really tried to find out what the various receivers really would enjoy.

2.3 *Satisfaction in response*

Does the student exhibit an emotional reaction when he performs a task? An affirmative answer to this question indicates the essential attainment of this level of affective behavior. The following *sentence completion* type of activity is a simple device for securing emotional responses.

"Respond *as quickly as possible* to the following unfinished sentences. Write the first thought that comes into your mind in the blank spaces."

Catcher in the Rye made me feel that ______________.
The saying, "Do unto others as you would have them do unto you" makes me want to ______________.
Shakespeare's sonnets ______________.
When I finished reading *Gone With The Wind*, I ______________.

3.0 Valuing

The individual develops criteria of worth for things, phenomena, and behaviors as a result of external and internal factors. Valuing has three subcategories which parallel the degrees or intensities in category 2.0 Responding. They are:

Subcategory	*Basic Affective Element*
3.1 Acceptance of a value	Belief—accepts value
3.2 Preference for a value	Identifies with value
3.3 Commitment	Conviction beyond doubt

Behaviors in this category are motivated not by the desire to obey or conform, but by the student's commitment to the underlying value guiding the behaviors.

3.1 *Acceptance of a value*

Beliefs have been defined as emotional acceptances of propositions or doctrines upon what one implicitly considers adequate grounds. At first, a belief is somewhat tenuous, as in this subcategory. However, there is a definite and clear positive statement that the values phenomenon has intrinsic worth beyond just simple satisfaction. The following *attitude rating scale*[10] helps the teacher see how the student feels about science.

Directions

Please place a check *anywhere* along the continuum of each of the two opposing words on a line to show how YOU feel about science.

---

10 Albert F. Eiss and Mary Blatt Harbeck, op. cit., p. 20.

SCIENCE IS

whee	yetch!
theoretical	practical
inconvenient	convenient
complex	simple
wide	narrow
easy	troublesome
unnecessary	basic
dull	emotional
efficient	inefficient
universal	limited
outgoing	ingrown
broadly interpretive	dogmatic
imaginative	unimaginative
interesting	uninteresting
objective	subjective
clear	fuzzy
useful	harmful
good	bad
exciting	boring

3.2 Preference for a value

At this level the student is willing not only to be identified with a value, but is committed enough to seek and pursue it. The *situational method* is a most appropriate one for eliciting preference for a value. In this method, a situation is structured in which a wide variety of choices are available to the student. The teacher is looking for a consistency of choices to confirm the student's preference for a value. Such a situation might be constructed as depicted below to see if the student has developed a preference for a nutritionally balanced diet. An observer could be posted at the end of the serving line in a cafeteria to note student food choices. The pattern of choices could then be analyzed by teacher.

Directions

During your regular noon meal, you may choose freely from a wide range of foods. However, your choices must be made within the regular price of ______ cents established by your student-faculty board. The student-faculty board has also provided an organically grown vegetarian menu for those who prefer to purchase these foods.*

Please select whatever *you* prefer to eat within the allotted price level set. Please keep a two-week log of your food choices. Thank you.

3.3 Commitment

This subcategory is the highest level of valuing. There is a tension at this stage that has these characteristics:

1. The valuing of an object or phenomenon endures over a period of time.
2. There must also be a considerable investment of energy in the object or phenomenon that is valued.
3. There should be actions in behalf of the value, belief or sentiment—actions which by their very nature imply a commitment.[11]

In order to elicit not only the student's belief but also information about his willingness to act upon that belief, the following questionnaire might be used:

Directions

Please describe briefly any *actions* you have taken on any topic listed below:

Writing Letters

1. Wrote a "Letter to the Editor" of the local newspaper.
2. Wrote a letter to my congressman or senator.
3. Wrote a letter to someone in the news who has done something I respect or admire.
4. Other (specify) ______________________________

* *Note:* High school and college students have shown increased interest in nutrition and especially in organically grown foods. Therefore, the above activity is very relevant for today's schools. The following brief, but well written, magazine article is recommended as it describes nutrition and organic foods free-selection experiments among students at the University of Santa Cruz in California, including the growing of organic foods by the students themselves: Elizabeth Lansing, "The Move to Eat Natural," *Life*, Vol. 64, No. 24 (December 11, 1970), pp. 44–52.

[11] David R. Krathwohl, et al., op. cit., p. 150.

Attended a Meeting or Organized One

1. Wrote a letter to one of the organizations working for a cause I believe in and asked to be put on their mailing list announcing their meetings. Attended them.
2. Scanned the newspapers for open meeting announcements of groups in which I am interested. Attend one.
3. Asked my own club, civic group, or church group to have a meeting or invite a guest speaker on a topic I am deeply concerned about.
4. Others (specify) ______________________

Took Part in Some Action

1. Distributed leaflets door-to-door or by standing at a bus or subway entrance.
2. Peacefully picketed.
3. Organized a petition drive.
4. Interviewed people who have influence in your town.
5. Wore a button.
6. Took part in a peaceful march or other demonstration.
7. Went to see some official about some issue as a member of a delegation.
8. Others (specify) ______________________

Face-to-Face Acts

1. Spoke up for *my* point of view. (For example, if someone says something derogatory about a race or a religion, you can tactfully talk to him about your point of view.)
2. Gave someone a pamphlet or an article which argues for a different position than he claims to hold.
3. Others (specify) ______________________[12]

The action inventory may not tell the teacher specifically what the learner's beliefs are. To accomplish this, the teacher or students might select a currently controversial issue and ask students what *actions* they might take in the situation. The issue could be one from school, local community, state, or national scene. The criteria for the selection of a controversial issue should be the degree to which the students identify with one side or another.

---

[12] Sidney B. Simon, "Your Values Are Showing," *Colloquy,* 3 (1), January, 1970, p. 32. Printed by permission of author and publisher: John Westerhoff, Editor, 1505 Race Street, Philadelphia, Pa. 19102.

4.0 Organization

This is the category where a *value system* begins to formulate for the student. Two subcategories characterize this value system building, each interrelated and dependent upon each other:

Subcategory	*Basic Affective Element*
4.1 Conceptualization of a value	How does value relate to ones already held?
4.2 Organization of a value system	Ordered relationships of values.

4.1 Conceptualization of a value

This subcategory permits the student to see how new value relates to those that he already holds, or to new ones that he is coming to hold. This process of conceptualization involves abstraction and generalizations. For this reason, it is largely cognitive, but value conceptualization could not have been undertaken without a great deal of affect having developed. An excellent device for evaluating the student's conceptualization of a value is what Louis E. Raths and his associates call the *Values Continuum.* The values continuum works like this:

> The class or the teacher identifies an issue to be discussed in class. It could be federal control of education, inter-scholastic sports, religious tolerance, censorship, socialized medicine, birth control, or anything else. Then two polar positions are identified, e.g., the federal government should control virtually everything a school does and the federal government should have no influence in what school does. These two positions, sometimes captured in argument from two newspapers or magazines, one reactionary and one radical, are placed at opposite ends of a line on the board, and the continuum is born. The task of the class, then, is to identify other positions in the issue and try to place them on the continuum, both in relationship to the poles and to positions already placed.
>
> Sometimes issues will be found which are multidimensional and, therefore, more than one long line is needed, but usually this is unnecessary. In any case, the importance of the value continuum is not in giving visual representation to an issue but

in showing the class that most issues have a wealth of possible alternatives, each of which has particular consequences.[13]

An example of a values continuum dealing with students' values concerning the draft might take this form:

Directions

Here are two extreme positions at either end of the draft continuum. At one extreme is Eager Egbert. He is so committed to the military that he has been trying to enlist since he was eleven. Now he is fourteen, and he is trying for the ninetieth time to look older so he can go to Vietnam and kill as many Viet Cong as possible.

At the other extreme is Maiming Malcolm. He borrows his father's shotgun and shoots off five toes so he will never have to be anything but 4F for the rest of his life.

Between these extremes is much room for diversity of opinion. Place *YOUR* name on the line which best describes where *YOU* fit. Be ready to defend *YOUR* position with how *YOU* arrived at that position.

Remember: There is no *right* answer. Keep in mind each individual's right of choice and the pluralism which made this society what it is today.[14]

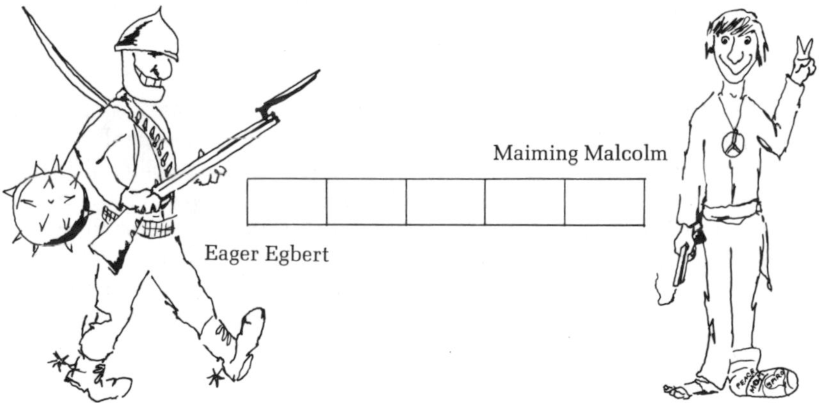

4.2 Organization of a value system

The student at this level brings together a complex of values into an ordered relationship of one value with another. Many

[13] Louis E. Raths, Merrill Harmin, and Sidney B. Simon, op. cit., p. 129.
[14] Sidney B. Simon, op. cit., p. 21.

inventories and schedules, which try to investigate aspects of personality, are also concerned with the person's pattern of values. Among the easily administered and scored devices useful to the teacher in this subcategory are:

Differential Value Profile, Walter L. Thomas, 3860 Plainfield, N.E., Grand Rapids, Michigan 49505.

Early School Personality Questionnaire, Richard W. Coan, University of Arizona, Tucson, Arizona, and Raymond B. Cattell, University of Illinois, Urbana, Illinois.

How I See Myself, Ira J. Gordon, College of Education, University of Florida, Gainesville, Florida 33601.

Index of Adjustment and Values, Robert E. Bills, College of Education, University of Alabama, Birmingham, Alabama.

Minnesota Multiphasic Personality Inventory, University of Minnesota Press, Minneapolis, Minnesota. 55414.

Pennsylvania Citizenship Assessment Instrument—Fifth Grade, Ernest L. Peters, Director, Division of Cooperative Research Services, Department of Public Instruction, Room 214, Executive House, Harrisburg, Pennsylvania 17126.

Personal Values Inventory, George E. Schlesser, 28 Payne Street, Hamilton, New York 13346.

The Projective Tests of Attitude, Lawrence F. Lowery, 4651 Tolman Hall, University of California, Berkeley, California 94720.

Scales for School and Law Attitudes, Nason Hall, Department of Sociology, The Ohio State University, Columbus, Ohio 43210.

Self-Social Symbols Tests (Preschool, Primary and Adult Forms), Edmund H. Henderson, The Reading Center, University of Delaware, Newark, Delaware, 19711.

School Attitude Q-Sort, William Frank Rowe, 487 Steeple Chase Lane, Somerville, New Jersey 08876.

The Sixteen Personality Factor Test, Raymond B. Cattell and H. W. Eber, IPAT, 1602-04 Coronado Drive, Champaign, Illinois.

Study of Values, Gordon W. Allport, Houghton Mifflin, Co., Boston, Mass.

Another way to assess how students see *each other* organizing and acting upon their value systems is to use simple *sociometric devices.* The following could be given to a class after they have been together long enough to know each other:

Directions

On this sheet are ten statements made by students your age. On the second sheet handed out to you is a list of names of all the students in this class. Please fill in the names *you* feel apply to each question. Please use all the names as many times as you feel they are applicable to different questions.

Who Is Like This?

1. I do not seem to be interested in anything. I sit quietly, dully, passively, bored much of the time in school and out of school. I don't care one way or the other. I am apathetic, *disinterested.*
   a. What students are VERY MUCH like this?
   b. What students are SOMEWHAT like this?

2. I am *flighty.* I am interested in a lot of things, but only for fleeting moments, then I get interested in something entirely different. I can get started, but I don't seem to follow through. I am attracted to a million things, but I don't stick with anything long enough to do something about it. I fly rapidly from his to that.
   a. What students are VERY MUCH like this?
   b. What students are SOMEWHAT like this?

3. I am considered *good-looking.* I look like people in movies or in pictures. Some people might call me handsome or beautiful.
   a. What students are VERY MUCH like this?
   b. What students are SOMEWHAT like this?

4. It's hard for me to make up my mind. I take a long time to make decisions. I am full of doubts. I am often *very uncertain.*
   a. What students are VERY MUCH like this?
   b. What students are SOMEWHAT like this?

5. I am *very inconsistent.* Today I may be for something, but tomorrow I may be against it. It's hard to tell what side I will be on. I say this, but I do that. Or sometimes I say one thing and then, later, say just the opposite.
   a. What students are VERY MUCH like this?
   b. What students are SOMEWHAT like this?

6. I just seem to drift. I go from here to there without having much to do with it. And I don't care much. I go the way events take me. I don't struggle. Some people might call me a *drifter.*
   a. What students are VERY MUCH like this?
   b. What students are SOMEWHAT like this?

7. I am *well-co-ordinated.* I may not be strong, but I can control my motions and can play sports very well. Some people say I am graceful. I am not at all clumsy.
   a. What students are VERY MUCH like this?
   b. What students are SOMEWHAT like this?

8. I like to *conform* to what is expected of me. I may conform to what a grown-up wants. I may conform to what other kids want. I may have one person to follow and I do whatever that person wants. But I don't much want to be independent. I like to follow someone else's lead.
   a. What students are VERY MUCH like this?
   b. What students are SOMEWHAT like this?

9. I am just the opposite of a conformer—I like to dissent, to argue with anyone and everyone, to take the opposite point of view. I seem to be against most everything. I like to argue, complain, *dissent.*
   a. What students are VERY MUCH like this?
   b. What students are SOMEWHAT like this?

10. I like to make believe that I am somebody else. I often *play roles,* pretending that I am somebody different, right in the classroom or outside. I like to act even when there is no play.
    a. What students are VERY MUCH like this?
    b. What students are SOMEWHAT like this?[15]

5.0 Characterization by a value or value complex

The student's value system is internalized to the point that he has his own unique personal characteristics and credo or principles and ideals. Krathwohl makes the point in this manner concerning the school's role in this final level of affective behavior:

> Realistically, formal education generally cannot reach this level, at least in our society. In all open and pluralistic societies, such as our own, the maturity and personal integration required at this level are not attained until at least some years after the individual has completed his formal education.[16]

[15] Louis E. Raths, et al., op. cit. pp. 179–180.
[16] David R. Krathwohl, et al., op. cit. p. 165.

The subcategories for this level are:

Subcategory	Basic Affective Elements
5.1 Generalized set	Internal consistency of value system
5.2 Characterization	World view or total philosophy of life

5.1 Generalized set

The student exhibits an internal consistency to his system of attitudes, beliefs, and values. In psychology this consistency might be called homeostasis or predisposition to act in a predictable way according to value system. *Projective techniques* are potentially useful for getting at this generalized set. The *Thematic Apperception Test* (TAT) is such a test as is the following one designed to test students' respect for the worth and dignity of human beings.

Problems in Human Relations Test[17]

1. Tom and Bob who know each other only slightly were double-dating two girls who were roommates. A sudden storm made it impossible to go to the beach as planned. Tom suggested going to a movie. After making the suggestion, he realized Bob was without funds. As Tom, what would you do?
   (1) Pay for the party.
   (2) Lend Bob money.
   (3) Leave it up to the girls.
   *(4) Get Bob to suggest something.
   (5) Apologize to Bob for making the suggestion.
2. Your social organization has pledged a student who is not liked by some of the members. One of your friends threatens to leave the social organization if this person is initiated. What would you do?
   (1) Talk to your friend.
   (2) Do not initiate the prospective member.
   (3) Get more members to support the prospective member.
   *(4) Vote on the prospective member.
   (5) Postpone the vote until the matter works itself out.

Scoring rationale: The response marked with an asterisk is keyed to a point of view which the authors of the instrument call "Democratic."

[17] Paul L. Dressel and Lewis B. Mayhew, *General Education, Explorations in Evaluation* (Washington, D.C.: American Council on Education, 1954), pp. 229–37.

5.2 Characterization

Here is the highest level of all affective behavior—a total value system encompassing a world-view or total philosophy of life. Few people achieve this level of humanitarianism such as exemplified by Lincoln, Gandhi, or Einstein. The *Projective techniques* mentioned previously in this category are useful in ferreting out students' feelings about conscience and democratic ideals. The teacher will find that he rarely if ever has any direct role in developing this level of affective behavior in his students.

FURTHER IMPLICATIONS OF AFFECTIVE DOMAIN FOR DEVELOPING QUESTIONING SKILLS

Teachers can and should develop skills for helping their students build viable value systems and positive affective behavior. The following are presented for your consideration and use in improving your techniques in using questioning in teaching:

I. *Address all of your teaching to real basic societal issues and controversies, with the inclusion of issues and values.* A joint Commission of the Association of Classroom Teachers of the National Education Association and the American Association for School Administrators support this and recommend: ". . . that schools should provide definite educational experiences which teach young people to develop viable values systems and standards for personal behavior."[18]

II. *Help students develop CRITERIA for constantly evaluating their values.*[19]

1. *THE value should be chosen freely without coercion and followed whether or not an authority is watching.*
   a. Where do you suppose you first got that idea?
   b. How long have you felt that way?
   c. What would people say if you weren't to do what you say you must do?
   d. Are you getting help from anyone? Do you need more help? Can I help?

---

[18] Reported in: *Phi Delta Kappan*, March 1970, p. 389.

[19] The categories of clarifying responses suggested by the seven valuing processes are taken from Louis E. Raths, et al., op. cit. pp. 63–65.

e. Are you the only one in your crowd who feels this way?
f. What do your parents want you to be?
g. Is there any rebellion in your choice?
h. How many years will you give to it? What will you do if you're not good enough?
i. Do you think the idea of having thousands of people cheering when you come out on the field has anything to do with your choice?

2. *Alternatives should be present from which the individual can choose and not just one choice.*

a. What else did you consider before you picked this?
b. How long did you look around before you decided?
c. Was it a hard decision? What went into the final decision? Who helped? Do you need any further help?
d. Did you consider another possible alternative?
e. Are there some reasons behind your choice?
f. What choices did you reject before you settled on your present idea or action?
g. What's really good about this choice which makes it stand out from the other possibilities?

3. *Choices should be made after thoughtful consideration of the consequences of each alternative.*

a. What would be the consequences of each alternative available?
b. Have you thought about this very much? How did your thinking go?
c. Is this what I understand you to say . . . [interpret his statement]?
d. Are you implying that . . . [distort his statement to see if he is clear enough to correct the distortion]?
e. What assumptions are involved in your choice. Let's examine them.
f. Define the terms you use. Give me an example of the kind of job you can get without a high-school diploma.
g. Now if you do this, what will happen to that?
h. Is what you say consistent with what you said earlier?
i. Just what is good about this choice?
j. Where will it lead?
k. For whom are you doing this?
l. With these other choices, rank them in order of significance.
m. What will you have to do? What are your first steps? Second steps?
n. Whom else did you talk to?
o. Have you really weighed it fully?

4. *The individual should prize, cherish, esteem and respect the choices he freely and thoughtfully makes.*

   a. Are you glad you feel that way?
   b. How long have you wanted it?
   c. What good is it? What purpose does it serve? Why is it important to you?
   d. Should everyone do it your way?
   e. Is it something you really prize?
   f. In what way would life be different without it?

5. *The individual is proud of and glad to be publically associated with his value and champions it.*

   a. Would you tell the class the way you feel some time?
   b. Would you be willing to sign a petition supporting that idea?
   c. Are you saying that you believe . . . [repeat the idea]?
   d. You don't mean to say that you believe . . . [repeat the idea]?
   e. Should a person who believes the way you do speak out?
   f. Do people know that you believe that way or that you do that thing?
   g. Are you willing to stand up and be counted for that?

6. *The individual is willing to act upon his value.*

   a. I hear what you are for; now, is there anything you can do about it? Can I help?
   b. What are your first steps, second steps, etc?
   c. Are you willing to put some of your money behind this idea?
   d. Have you examined the consequences of your act?
   e. Are there any organizations set up for the same purposes? Will you join?
   f. Have you done much reading on the topic? Who has influenced you?
   g. Have you made any plans to do more than you already have done?
   h. Would you want other people to know you feel this way? What if they disagree with you?
   i. Where will this lead you? How far are you willing to go?
   j. How has it already affected your life? How will it affect it in the future?

7. *The value reappears on a number of occasions in the individual's life so that it forms a pattern of values.*

   a. Have you felt this way for some time?
   b. Have you done anything already? Do you do this often?
   c. What are your plans for doing more of it?
   d. Should you get other people interested and involved?

e. Has it been worth the time and money?
f. Are there some other things you can do which are like it?
g. How long do you think you will continue?
h. What did you *not* do when you went to do that? Was that o.k.?
i. How did you decide which had priority?
j. Did you run into any difficulty?
k. Will you do it again?

III. *Present ALL subject matter areas in such a manner that students investigate content and issues on these three levels:*

First—FACTS LEVEL
Second—CONCEPTS LEVEL
Third—VALUES LEVEL

Here is an example of three levels of science subject matter content but it could be in the social studies, language, or mathematics areas as well. Note the teacher questions under each of the three levels.

The Earth's Crust

Level I (Facts)

1. What are the three major groups of rocks?
2. Name three ways water can change the earth's surface.
3. What precious gems are found among the minerals in the earth?
4. How are volcanoes formed?
5. Etc., etc.

Level II (Concepts)

1. Show how two recent dramatic changes of the earth's surface were similar to changes which took place a million or more years ago.
2. Compare and contrast two theories of how mountains were formed. Which do you accept? Give your reasons.
3. Discuss the similarities and differences between precious and semi-precious stones, from a scientific point of view (as opposed to a young bride's point of view).
4. Where on the earth's surface are volcanoes most likely to occur today? Why?
5. Etc., etc.

Note: It is important to realize that just because questions at Levels I and II recognize an application in today's world, they do not automatically become Level III material. There needs to be a real connection with the students' lives, attitudes, and feelings for the questions to be raised to the third level, the values level.

Level III (Values)

1. Are you someone who is likely to become a rock hound some day?
2. Are the mountains a place where you really like to spend your vacations?
3. Where do you stand on oil companies' getting a depletion allowance?
4. In some states, strip miners find it cheaper to pay the fine than to do the reforestation the law requires. What is your reaction to this? What other information do you feel you need to know about this?
5. Which, if any, of these worry you at all or more than others?
   a. Converting the Florida Everglades into housing for senior citizens.
   b. Bulldozing a mountain so a four-lane road can go by.
   c. The cities spreading out over the earth's surface, leaving less and less open space.
6. When you get married, do you think you will give an expensive ring to your wife, or if you are a girl, do you think you will want one? Can you think of any alternative ways a husband might show affection for his bride?
7. Grass is too hard to maintain in a city; cities should be all asphalt. Do you agree or disagree? Give your reasons.
8. How do you think you would have answered these questions last year? Describe how your answers have changed, if they have.[20]
9. Etc., etc.

IV. *In any problem-situation designed to practice value clarification, the following kinds of open-ended questions can be asked:*[21]

---

[20] Earth's Crust example modified from materials appearing in Merrill Harmin, Howard Kirchenbaum, and Sidney B. Simon, "Teaching Science with a Focus On Values," *The Science Teacher,* Vol. 37, No. 1 (January, 1970), pp. 16–20.

[21] For a fuller explanation of these questions and their role in helping students develop value systems see Nancy W. Bauer, "Can You Teach Values?" *The Instructor* (August/September, 1970), pp. 37–38.

Observation or Data Gathering

What happened?
What did each person involved think?
What did each do?
Did anything else happen?

Analysis

What makes this a problem?
Do we need any more information?
What do other people think about the problem?
What might make them think so?

Synthesis

What do you think is the most important issue in the problem situation?

Alternatives

What might the people involved do?
What would you do in a similar situation?

Predicting Consequences

What probably would happen if each alternative was carried out?

Noting Values

What value is strengthened by each alternative?
What differences does it make what solution is chosen?
Who is affected by the chosen action?

V. *Wherever possible, try to use peer or peer group as the source of value-oriented facts instead of teacher or other adult authority because:*

> It is a well-known trait of young people that they tend to reject value-oriented facts when these are presented by parents, teachers, or other "authority figures." Coming from adults, such material is considered to be "preaching." In contrast, the same ideas are likely to be accepted without prejudice when the source is a peer or peer group.[22]

---

[22] For an excellent short description of the application of this quote to the structuring of anti-smoking education in Quincy, Massachusetts, by lecture-demonstrations by high school students, the reader is urged to see William H. O'Kane, "Peer Group Presents Value-Oriented Concepts," *The Science Teacher*, Vol. 37, No. 9 (December, 1970), pp. 17–18.

SUMMARY

The Affective Domain is concerned with the emotions of the learner—his interests, attitudes, values, and appreciations. The relationship between the cognitive and affective domain was explored. Reasons were presented for the slowness in development of teaching objectives and techniques for the affective domain. Definitions were given for all five of the categories of the affective domain with their corresponding subcategories. Suggestions for developing and assessing student's skills in the affective domain were presented in teacher questions and other teaching techniques.

6

QUESTIONING FOR CREATIVITY

One of the most human talents is creative talent. Being human is being creative. Creativity separates us from lower animals and when manifested swells our self-concept. To be creative is to be thrilled by learning of our potential capabilities as a person. Developing creative potential opens us to increasing experience; the more we are involved in creative enterprise, the more creative we become. An awareness that we are creative builds our "self-image," makes us more secure as individuals, broadens our vistas, opens us to new experiences. Not having opportunities for creative expression reduces our potential and has deleterious effects upon mental health.

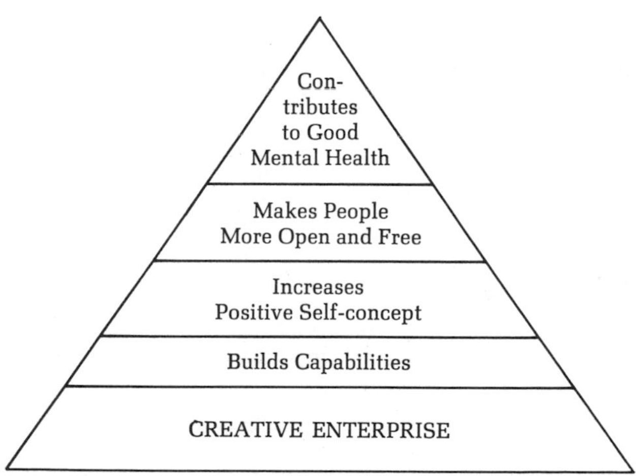

WHEN IS A PERSON CREATIVE?

A person is creative when he uses his mind to produce something uniquely new to him. It may be a sketch, sonata, song, phrase, poem, story, mathematical process, idea, or any new mental synthesis. When individuals are creative they are usually involved in one of the following processes:

1. Originate problems
2. Design methods for solving problems
3. Hypothesize or perform hypothetical deductive reasoning
4. Test hypotheses
5. Infer
6. Produce original artistic works
7. Communicate in a unique way
8. Evaluate and come up with better approaches to problems
9. Perceive hidden relations
10. Invent new uses for objects
11. Are resourceful and develop new approaches

Paul Torrance, a leader in research in creativity says: "I have chosen to define creative thinking as the process of sensing gaps or disturbing missing elements; forming ideas of hypotheses concerning them; testing these hypotheses and communicating the results, possibly modifying and retesting the hypotheses."[1]

HOW DO YOU IDENTIFY VERY CREATIVE PEOPLE?

All individuals have creative potential. Much of this potential remains quiescent because of a non-stimulating environment. Teachers have traditionally thought academic and creative talent correlated well, but, this is not true. For example, Paul Torrance says:

> Traditional tests of intelligence are heavily loaded with tasks requiring recognition, memory, and convergent thinking. . . . In fact, if we were to identify children on the basis of intelligence tests, we would eliminate from consideration ap-

[1] Paul Torrance, *Guiding Creative Talent* (Englewood Cliffs, N.J.: Prentice Hall, Inc., 1962), p. 16.

> proximately seventy percent of the most creative. This percentage seems to hold fairly well, no matter what educational level we study, from kindergarten through graduate school.[2]

Dr. Calvin Taylor, another renowned researcher in creativity, has come to similar conclusions. He says:

> Persons with equal grade point averages or with equal I.Q. scores can differ widely in their degree of creativeness. In other words, the I.Q. talent (or the closely related academic talent) is one important type of giftedness, but certainly not the only type. The creative individual presents a second type—a new portrait in giftedness—and tests that are quite different from current intelligence tests are typically used in searches for the creatives. Imitative processes are not the same as creative processes, nor are the good learner and the creative producer necessarily the same person, because *receiving and producing* existing knowledge—knowledge that someone else has earlier produced—is a different psychological process from *thinking and producing* something new of your own.[3]

Academic Talent *Receiving and Reproducing*	*Creative Talent* *Thinking and Producing*

Creative individuals may be recognized by the following characteristics:

1. Life history of encouraging creative response
2. Curious
3. Venturesome—likes to discover
4. Self-sufficient and independent
5. Prefers difficult tasks and challenges
6. Nonconforms
7. Enjoys solving problems
8. Flexible thinker
9. Fluent, gives rapid and unexpected answers to questions
10. Demonstrates ability to synthesize and sees implications
11. Usually well read
12. Likes variety and the revising of things

[2] *Ibid.*, pp. 4–5.

[3] Calvin Taylor, "Accent on Talent," NEA Journal, Vol. 1 No. 1 (September, 1966), p. 1.

Do not assume that a student who demonstrates one or two of the above characteristics is necessarily a very creative person. However, if you do perceive a manifestation of some of these, you should be alert for other clues to determine whether or not the student has the potential to become an outstandingly creative individual.

SCHOOLS NEED TO GIVE MORE ATTENTION TO DEVELOPING CREATIVE TALENT

What if you had been exposed to teachers whose fundamental purpose had been to help you manifest your creative potential? How creative would you be today? Certainly, you would be more creative than you are now.

Traditionally, schools have not done an outstanding job in stimulating creative talent. Dr. Donald McKennon, for example, in studying outstanding professionally creative adults, found the majority received *C*s and *B*s in school, not *A*s.[4] Compare the recognition given athletes to that of creative individuals in schools. If equal amount of faculty time and recognition were devoted to creative achievement and athletics, the manifestation of student creativity undoubtedly would increase to a greater degree than is presently the case.

How to stimulate creative enterprise

Granted that the fully functioning person is a creative person, how can you insure students are given opportunities to be creative? Primarily, you must insure that the learning environment is student-centered rather than teacher-centered. Students should be free to express their feelings. Give them opportunities and freedom to work. Encourage creative enterprise, and give recognition for creative achievement. Try to be involved in less teacher talk; listen more, and allow students to use you, other students, and

---

[4] Donald McKennon, "The Creative Individual," Broadcast #50250 V. E. Columbia Broadcasting System, University of California Explorer (Unpublished, January 28, 1962).

groups as sounding boards for their ideas. The types of questions you ask in your assignments play a big part. There should be less emphasis on questioning for the right answer and more open-ended divergent types of involvement. Questions requiring students to respond in the manner indicated on the first page of this chapter (i.e., originating problems, inferring, etc.) lead to creative endeavor.

Shown below is a suggested format for questions requiring creative responses.

Creative Response Questions Format

Process	*Question*
1. Evaluate	What is your reaction to: a play, concert, story, social event, etc.?
2. Evaluate	If you were going to make something better, i.e., a play, car, couch, skis, bicycle, painting, poem, experiment, solve a problem, what changes would you make?
3. Design an approach to solve a problem	a. How would you go about solving this problem? b. In what ways would you artistically convey your feelings about . . . the film, play, picture, painting, course problem? c. What picture would you draw to show what science, mathematics, home economics, or social studies means to you?
4. Design an experiment	How would you design an experiment to find an answer to the problem?
5. Hypothesize	What do you think will happen if . . . ?
6. Test hypotheses	Which of these hypotheses is best, and why?

Process	*Question*
7. Infer	What inferences and conclusions can you make from the statement: People who smoke have more lung cancer than people who do not smoke? What inferences can you make from these statements? (1) Smoking causes lung cancer. (2) People who smoke have a biological susceptibility to lung cancer.
8. Invent	How many ways can you think of using a tin can, clothes hanger, roller skates, spool of thread, cardboard box, can opener, surfboard, etc.?
9. Invent	What things do you think are most in need of invention?
10. Design an approach to solve a problem	If you were going to teach________ to the class below you, how would you do it to insure they really learned?
11. Design an approach to solve a problem	If you were going to convey in an artistic way the message of peace, Christmas, good will to men, non-smoking, non-use of drugs, etc., what would you do?
12. Design an approach to solve a problem	What kinds of problems should we study?
13. Infer	How are the plays, animals, problems, etc., alike or dissimilar?

The above list is by no means complete. You should attempt to build your own creative question format list for your class or academic discipline. The construction of this list will involve creative enterprise and give you, as a result, better insights into developing good questioning techniques. The more you evaluate and attempt to construct questions for creativity, the better you will get and the greater fun you will have.

Some instructors, particularly on the junior and senior high school levels, have taught students to formulate creative questions by defining creativity, showing the format for creative questions such as outlined above, and then having students write creative questions. Students also can be encouraged to add to the creative questioning format list. This type of involvement has been found to be very successful with high school students and involves them in an investigation of the subject matter in a unique way.

Remember, almost all educational aids—films, tapes, books, pictures, etc.—can be adapted for creative ends even though they were not designed specifically for this purpose. To prove this to yourself, look at some traditional assignment you have given requiring no creative production. Modify it by writing questions as suggested above. In most cases you will be successful in constructing a more creative activity and gain confidence in devising an educational environment for stimulating the manifestation of a very valuable human talent. Listed below are examples of questions, in addition to those mentioned above, that can be used with a film or modified slightly for filmstrip or 35mm slide presentations.

1. If you were going to change this film for greater impact, what would you do to it?
2. If you were going to convey the message of this film in an artistic manner to a bedridden student in his home, what would you do?
3. (The teacher stops the film and then asks)
   a. What do you think the next scene will be and why?
   b. If you were going to finish the film, what would you do and why?
   c. If you were going to change or add music to the film, what would you choose and why?
   d. If you were going to write a short poem to be included in the film at this point, what would it be?
4. How would you change the title to make it more interesting?
5. How would you change the ending to produce a better effect?

SUMMARY

One of the most human talents is creative talent. It differentiates man from the lower animals, contributes to a person's mental health, and encourages a positive self-concept. Creativity may involve originating a problem, designing approaches to solve problems, formulating and testing hypotheses, inferring, communicating, evaluating techniques and problem solving approaches, inventing, and demonstrating resourcefulness.

Although all individuals have some creative talent, the outstanding creative person is more curious, venturesome, self-sufficient, prefers difficult tasks, nonconforms, enjoys solving problems, is more flexible and fluent in thinking, and likes variety and revising things.

Schools generally have not done an outstanding job of rewarding creative enterprise. It is, therefore, extremely important that teachers concentrate on creative questioning techniques. They should give students more opportunities to originate and solve problems, hypothesize about solutions to problems, demonstrate fluency and flexibility of ideas, invent, evaluate solutions, and create artistic works. Creative questioning should permeate the entire instructional environment, including discussions, evaluations, and audio-visual aids. Formats to use as guides to follow in writing creative questions are provided in the chapter.

7

CONSTRUCTING TEACHING LESSONS USING A DISCOVERY QUESTIONING APPROACH

Generally speaking, any of the questioning techniques outlined in previous chapters can be adapted to various instructional media and methods of teaching. In doing this you should keep in mind three general principles when starting questioning:

1. Ask divergent questions
2. Avoid the overuse of questions requiring only memory responses
3. Involve each student in the questioning process as much as possible.

Outlined below are several suggestions to use in writing questions for various instructional approaches. While reading these, think of ways you might use them in your own classes.

USING FILMS

Most instructors use a film by showing it in entirety and then covering the most salient points in discussion. This is good because it helps to clarify and reinforce the film's valuable instructional aspects.

However, another way of using a film that is more likely to involve students is to stop it several times during the showing. Each time it is stopped, the instructor should ask pertinent quesions about what was portrayed in the previous sequence. An instructor can also ask the class occasionally why they think he stopped the film where he did, and then proceed with a regular sequence of inquiry oriented questions.

An alternate technique of using a film is to stop it at various places and have students answer written questions handed out to them. After the students have written their answers, the instructor may call upon various students to read what they wrote and have other members of the class respond to these answers. This procedure may be done several times throughout the showing. Refer to Chapter 6 for specific suggestions on how to write questions which will supplement the use of a film in a creative way.

The one word or picture approach

Another use of a film is to stop it several times and ask students to write one word or draw a picture of what it means to them. At the conclusion of the film, students may be asked to write their words on the chalkboard. They are encouraged either to tell or write a story about the film using as many of these words as possible. A similar approach may be used by having the various members of the class display their drawings and discuss them, or write below their pictures what the film meant to them. The pictures may be posted on a bulletin board.

Filmstrips

Most of the above procedures for using films are also good with filmstrips. It is especially important to discuss the filmstrip as you progress through it. You should try to use inquiry discussion techniques as much as possible. Some general questions you might ask are:

1. What questions can you ask about this scene?
2. What is the significance of this picture?
3. How is it related to the previous one?
4. If you were going to say one word about the picture, what would it be?
5. If you were going to write an inquiry type question about this picture, what would you write?
6. If you were going to improve this picture and/or filmstrip, or make one to replace it, what would you do?

7. If you were going to put music with this picture and/or filmstrip, what would you select and why?
8. If you were going to construct a poem to go with this picture and/or filmstrip, what would it be?
9. How does this picture make you feel?
10. How do the people feel as depicted in this picture?
11. Now that you have seen this filmstrip, what do you think the next filmstrip should contain?
12. How do you think this filmstrip should be used so that you would get more out of it?

35mm slides and Polaroid camera

The procedures outlined above may also be used with a series of 35mm slides or Polaroid photographs. Students should be encouraged to make their own pictures, devise questions to go with them, and present these to their class.

Film loop

The questions asked in the filmstrip section above may also be used with film loops. For example, in science, social studies, or mathematics, students may be presented a problem in the first part of the loop and then asked how they would go about solving it. After discussing their ideas, the loop is continued and they are given further information. They may be asked to interpret data which will provide conclusions or they might be asked to make suggestions about improving procedures used in solving the problem.

Most film loops have not been designed for discovery or inquiry teaching, but they can be easily adapted for this purpose by constructing a series of inquiry questions to go wtih them. One procedure that has been successful with junior and senior high school students is for the instructor to show a few loops demonstrating an inquiry approach. After students understand how to use the loops in an inquiry manner, they are assigned to groups to view loops and construct questions to go with them to be shown later to the rest of the class. After the class has seen the loops and answered the questions, they should be invited to evaluate the questions of the groups and suggest modifications.

USING TAPES

Taping and replaying a class discussion

Tape recorders provide a number of ways of involving students in investigative activities. Cassette recorders, because of their ease of operation and economy, generally are better to use than the more conventional machines. One approach to their use is to tape a class discussion and replay parts or all of it. While hearing the tape, the students should analyze the types of questions asked and the appropriateness of their own responses. The tape may be stopped periodically to discuss answers and comments.

The replaying of a discussion may also be used to help students who have missed a class because of absence. They can come in, at their leisure, to listen to the recorder and give their impression of the significance of the discussion. They should be encouraged to write questions they think might have been introduced in it.

Taping questions for media

As suggested above, questions may be taped to go with various instructional media. These questions can be listened to by individual students using headsets, in study carrols, or by an entire class.

Taping test questions

Taping questions for tests is particularly effective for students having difficulty with reading. Students may be given a test sheet containing a series of drawings or diagrams. The tape recorder is then turned on and they are asked questions related to their test. More is said about this under the section on evaluation in this chapter.

STUDENT QUESTIONS

Students should be given a topic to study and then asked to formulate questions about it. This activity works particularly well if students are divided into small groups and encouraged to produce instructional materials to be shown to their class using the following: music, poetry, 35mm slides, transparencies, 8mm film, a series of diagrams, photographs, or pictures placed on poster board. Polaroid cameras can be used effectively for this purpose. Students often have them available at home and are willing to use the camera for instructional purposes when requested.

The advantage of student involvement in making learning aids is that it allows them to manifest a greater number of talents, including creativity, social interaction, organizaiton, communication, and responsibility, and develop their critical thinking by formulating good questions.

PICTORIAL RIDDLES

Pictorial riddles are riddles presented to the class in picture or diagram form, depicting some novel or discrepant event. A discrepant event is one that presents an inconsistency between what the student believes reasonably should happen and what actually takes place. Pictorial riddles may be prepared by using the following:

1. Diagrams
2. Pictures from magazines
3. Photographs
4. Polaroid pictures
5. Transparencies
6. Drawings made on the chalkboard.

Riddles may illustrate an actual or gimmicked situation. In the gimmicked situation, students are asked questions as to what is wrong with what they see. In the first example below, a discrepant event is presented. In one of the other examples, the riddle presents a gimmicked situation and the pupils are supposed to state what is wrong. See if you can identify the gimmicked riddle.

Science

1. What do you observe?
2. What can be done with this swinging wonder?
3. What questions can you ask about the toy?

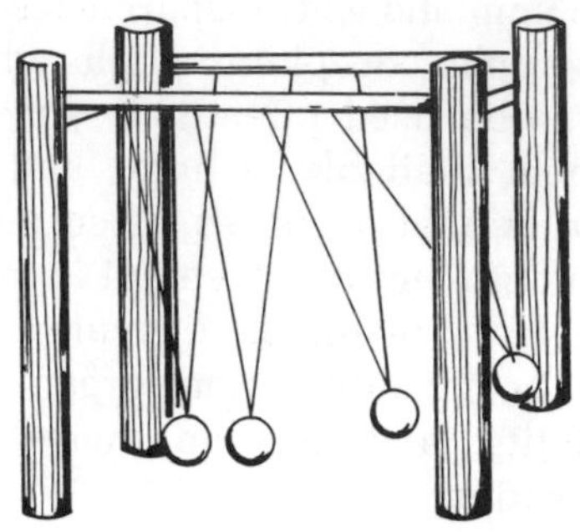

4. What will happen if one ball is pulled up and let go?
5. What will happen if a ball is pulled up and then slammed down against another ball?
6. Knowing what you do about how this toy operates, in what ways can you apply this information to your life?
7. What inventions could you make using this toy?

Social Science or History

1. What questions can you ask about the castle?
2. What kind of social structure do you think these people had? Why?
3. What did the castle represent to people who lived near it?
4. If you were going to provide better security for people, what would you do?
5. Why aren't castles built today?
6. What has replaced the castle in our society?
7. How has security been modified from the days of castles?

Mathematics

1. What do you notice about the above shapes?
2. How do the shapes vary?
3. On what shape would you like to be placed and why?
4. Which shapes are open?
5. Which shapes are closed?
6. What shapes would you make that would be like these but different?

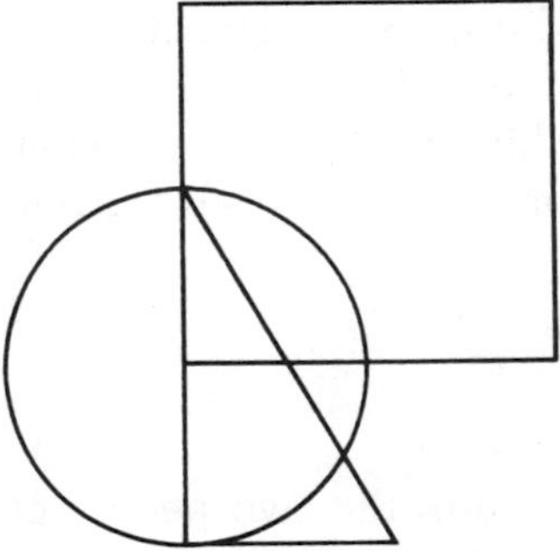

1. What kinds of questions could you ask about this diagram?
2. How would you go about answering these questions?

Driver Education

1. What do you notice about this accident?
2. Name all the things you can that could have contributed to the accident?
3. State several ways this accident could have been prevented?
4. What do you think happened to the occupants of the car?
5. How could the car's construction be improved to better protect the occupant?
6. How do you think you would have behaved as a driver during the time of the accident's occurrence?

English

1. What do you think the two people on page 123 feel?
2. What do you feel about these people?
3. How would you feel if you were in one of their places?

4. If you wanted to produce a photograph to illustrate how you feel today, what kind of photograph would you make?

(If possible, give the students Polaroid cameras and let them produce pictures illustrating their feelings.)

Art

1. What is good about this art?
2. What could be improved about it?
3. If you were going to change it, what would you do?
4. What were your feelings when you first looked at it?
5. What do you feel after you have looked at it a while?
6. What would happen if you changed its texture, color, etc.?

Homemaking

1. What do you notice about this cake?
2. How could this have happened?
3. How could it have been prevented?
4. If you want to insure the baking of a good cake, what should you do?

INVITATION TO DISCOVER

An invitation to discover is a discussion-type lesson written specifically to help individuals learn the techniques (i.e. critical thinking processes and procedures) of discovery. The fundamental purpose of the invitation is not to teach subject matter but to involve students in learning how to use their minds to make discoveries. Generally, however, invitations are constructed to go with subject matter related to a specific unit under study.

A typical invitation presents a problem to the student and through carefully designed questions invites him to devise a method to solve it, make hypotheses, draw conclusions from data, interpret data, or identify factors involved in the problem. Invitations can be written for various levels of learning. They may be presented in written form for students to read and respond to or given to small or large groups. Shown below is an example of an invitation; on the left margin are directions to follow in writing an invitation.

Invitation

What should be done to improve the community?

Directions

1. State the problem.	A wealthy man wanted to do something to improve the quality of life in a community. If you were this individual, what would you do and why?

Directions

2. Allow for discussion.	
3. You might record the suggestions on the chalkboard.	
4. After the discussion goes on for some time ask:	Of the suggestions just made, which is the best and why?
5. Give further information.	This man suggested to the city council that a park be built near the city hall for all of the people of the community to use.
6. Ask:	How do you think the city council reacted to his suggestion and why?
7. Give further information.	The city council turned down his proposal.
8. Ask:	Why?
9. Give further information.	They turned it down because there was no provision made for the upkeep of the park.
10. Ask:	What do you think of their decision now and why?
11. Ask:	If you were on the city council, what would you suggest the man do with his money?
12. Give further information.	One member of the city council suggested that this money be put to a better use by contributing to enlarging the badly over-crowded local hospital. Another city councilman thought the money should be used to buy several new books for the city library. A third member believed that the money should build a smaller park and some of it should be set aside to provide for upkeep.

Directions

13. Ask:	If you were the wealthy man, what would you do and why?
14. Ask:	How could you be certain that this would be the best way to help your community?
15. Ask:	When individuals propose suggestions for improving our school or community, what should be known before making a decision?

Suggestions for writing invitations

1. Prior to the time you write an invitation, ask students what kinds of problems concern them.
2. Accept and record all of the problems they suggest. Use these as a basis for invitations.
3. Select the content you wish to discuss.
4. Select the critical thinking processes you wish to have students involved in as outlined in previous sections of this book, i.e., hypothesizing, designing a way to solve a problem, inferring, etc.
5. Design a problem related to the objectives you outlined in steps 1 and 2. Ideas for invitations may be suggested from current magazines, newspapers, etc. For example, you might want to construct problems involving drugs, pollution, population, lack of humanism in the school, racial bias, etc.
6. Construct a series of questions requiring suggestions for solving the problem, making hypotheses, analyzing, recording, interpreting data, etc.
7. You should write each invitation as a series of steps. Information should be inserted at appropriate places to aid students' progress towards solving the problem. For example, you might present a problem involving racial discrimination in the school system. Have the class discuss what they think should be done. Then, give information about what a school district actually did. Then, ask what they think happened because of the district's plan. After dis-

cussing this point, give them further information on what happened and ask for conclusions, etc.

8. Present the problem for discussion.

DISCOVERY BULLETIN BOARDS

Bulletin board displays, like other instructional aids, can be designed as exciting inquiry-oriented investigations. These boards should become an integral part of the instructional system. The degree to which students become involved in them is determined by their maturation and the divergence of the questions asked. Listed below are suggestions for developing an inquiry-oriented bulletin board:

1. Determine what objectives you wish to develop with the board.
2. Collect pictures or make diagrams to help reach the objectives.
3. Invite students to help construct the bulletin board. Have them suggest questions to go with the diagrams, etc. If you do not wish to invite students to do the construction, outline in diagram form the bulletin board and prepare divergent questions to go with it.
4. Prepare the lettering and paste the pictures and diagrams on colored paper.
5. Have students make the bulletin board following the diagram you constructed.
6. After the purpose of the board has been served, have some students take it down and place it in a folder containing the diagram outlining its arrangement for future use.
7. List any possible modifications that should be made, particularly in the questions for next year.
8. The next time you use the display, modify it as suggested from the previous evaluation.

DISCOVERY AND INQUIRY

Designing Activities

Students may be involved in discovery to varying degrees. In *guided* discovery, the student is provided with considerable structure in order to assure that he has success in discovering some concept or principle. In *free* discovery or inquiry activities, the student is given relatively little guidance. He is asked to identify a problem to investigate or given one to study. For example he may be given a worm, snail, chemical compound, collection of electrical apparatus, or a social or mathematical problem and asked to find out as much as possible about it during the time allotted.

Designing guided discovery activities requires considerable questioning sophistication to prepare the study guides for the students. At first, it would seem free inquiry or discovery situations would require less questioning ability by the instructor, but this certainly is not the case. As students become involved and experience difficulty in making progress in their investigations, the instructor will probably have to come to their aid. He has to know how to ask just the right question to help them move towards the resolution of their problem without depriving them of opportunities to use their minds.

In both types of discovery or inquiry approaches, it is strongly recommended that the teacher, prior to the period of instruction, outline the types of questions he thinks will help guide students in solving the problem. Many of the questions you outline for the free discovery situation probably will never be used by you in teaching. However, because of your questioning pre-planning, you will most assuredly have a more relevant reservoir of questions to ask than has an instructor who does not think through the lessons he designs.

If an instructor is not well versed in teaching by discovery, it is suggested that he first try to use the guided discovery approach and write several discovery activities. When he first writes these he will find it takes considerable time. This is so because he has to develop his questioning ability and learn simultaneously how to structure a discovery activity. After writing a few of these, the time required is shortened and the instructor comprehends to a far better degree the role of critical questioning in the teaching process.

The following lessons are specifically designed for science laboratory activities; however, the format can be adapted for other subject areas such as mathematics, social studies, health, physical education, etc.

The general format of a guided discovery teaching laboratory lesson

A guided discovery teaching laboratory lesson consists of two parts. One part constructed mainly for the instructor, and the other is for the students as indicated below:

For the Instructor

1. Statement of the problem to be investigated (this may also be included in the lab sheet given to the student)
2. Grade level range
3. Principle(s) and concept(s) to be learned
4. Materials needed
5. Discussion questions

The Pupil Laboratory Sheet

1. Pupil discovery activities
2. Critical thinking processes
3. Open-ended (divergent) questions
4. Teacher's notes.

Refer to the lessons below and analyze how they are constructed. Then turn to the directions of how to write them.

Examples of Guided Discovery Lessons

Problem: HOW DOES AIR PRESSURE MOVE AN OBJECT?

Grade level: 6-11

Concepts

1. Air exerts pressure.
2. Gases expand when heated.
3. In order for paper to burn, there must be oxygen present.
4. When paper is burned, oxygen combines with Carbon and Hydrogen in the paper to produce carbon dioxide gas and water vapor.

Materials

Milk bottle or a bottle with a narrow neck
Peeled hard-boiled egg
Paper
Matches and candle

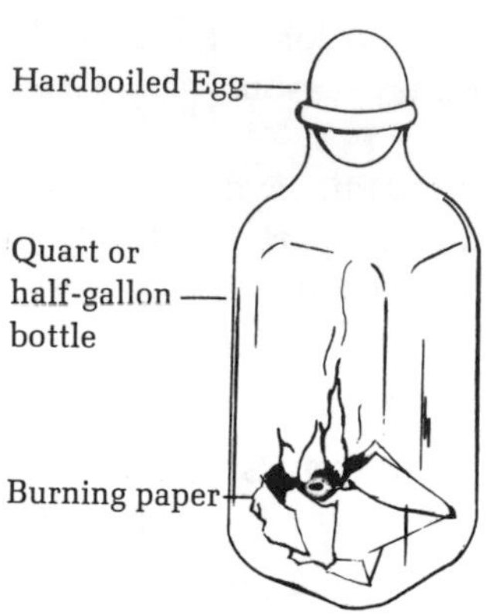

Discussion Questions

(critical thinking processes)

Comparing	How does the air pressure in a milk bottle compare to the air pressure in the room?
Hypothesizing	What would happen if you placed a hard-boiled egg in the neck of the bottle at room temperature?
Hypothesizing	What do you think would happen to the egg if you were able to decrease the amount of air pressure in the bottle?
Designing an Investigation	How would you decrease the air pressure in the bottle?

Student Discovery Activity

(Critical thinking processes)

Following directions	Obtain a milk bottle, a peeled hard-boiled egg, a piece of paper, and some matches.
Hypothesizing	What do you think will happen, if you light a piece of paper, drop it into the bottle, and then place an egg on the opening of the bottle?

Following directions	Light the edge of a piece of paper with a match or candle. Once the paper starts to burn, let it drop into the bottle.
Following directions	Allow the paper to burn for several seconds.
Following directions	Set the hard-boiled (peeled) egg in the opening of the bottle.
Hypothesizing	Why did you put the paper in the bottle and light it?
Applying	What does the paper need from the air in order to burn?
Applying	Since you don't destroy matter (in this case, oxygen), what happened to the oxygen that was used?
Inferring	What happens to air when it is heated?
Inferring	What happens to air in a room which is heated?
Inferring	Where is a room generally the coldest?
Inferring	How is the expansion or contraction of air affected?
Inferring	If warm air changes with an increase in temperature what happens to the air pressure in the bottle while the paper burns?
Inferring	Would there be more or less air in the jar immediately after the paper burned? Why?
Inferring	Why was it necessary to place the egg in the bottle *after* the paper burned for a while?
Applying	What happens to air as it cools?
Comparing	How did the air pressure in the room compare to the air pressure in the bottle after the air cooled in the bottle?
Observing	What happened to the egg?
Inferring	What caused the egg to move the way it did?

Designing an investigation	How could you get the egg out of the bottle without breaking the bottle?
Following directions	Turn the bottle upside down so that the egg falls into the opening.
Hypothesizing	What do you think will happen if you blow hard into the bottle?
Following directions	Blow hard into the bottle.
Following directions	Quickly take the jar away from your mouth.
Observing	What happened to the egg?
Inferring	What were you doing to the air pressure in the bottle when you blew into it?
Inferring	What caused the egg to move the way it did?

Open-ended Questions

Applying	1. Why do you often see this warning on a spray can? DO NOT PLACE THIS CAN IN FIRE OR NEAR HEAT.
Applying	2. What causes the tires in a car to hold their shape?
Designing an investigation	3. If you wanted to measure approximately how much the air pressure changes in the time you burn the paper in the bottle, how would you do it?
Designing an investigation	4. What other investigations could you do to determine what factors influence the rate at which the egg passes into the milk bottle?

Teacher's Explanation: When the paper burns it produces heat causing the air within the jar to expand, and some of it, as a consequence, escapes from the bottle. It is for this reason that the paper should be allowed to burn a few seconds before placing the egg on the bottle. Shortly after the flame goes out, the air inside the bottle begins to cool and contract, resulting in less air pressure. Since there is less air pressure in the bottle, the egg is pushed into the bottle by the greater air pressure in the room.

Problem: HOW DO A COCOON AND A POLLIWOG CHANGE?

Grade Level: (2-4)

Concepts

1. Some animals change in shape and size as they mature.
2. Some small animals have a heart.
3. Growing and developing animals may not look like their adult parents.
4. Animals need oxygen in order to live.

Materials

Cocoons of the different moths (these can be obtained from Turtox Biological Supply House or the children can be encouraged to collect them)
Razor blade, single edged
Jar, covered, with air holes in the lid
Large mayonnaise jar or aquarium
Paper
Polliwogs
Green aquatic plants or algae

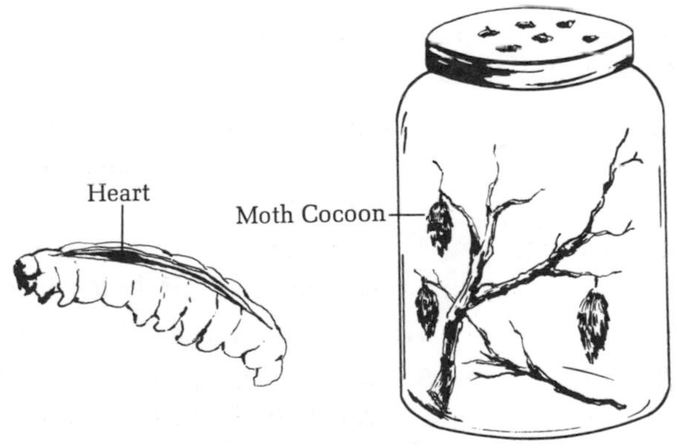

Discussion Questions

(Critical thinking processes)

Summarizing — How do animals change as they grow and develop?

Summarizing	How do humans change as they grow and develop?
Summarizing	How does a moth change as it grows and develops?
Designing an investigation	How could we find out?
Summarizing	How does a frog develop
Designing an investigation	How could we find out?

Student Discovery Activity

(Critical thinking processes)

Part I *Cocoon*

Teacher's Note: This activity should be done in groups of three.

Following directions	1. Obtain a single-edged razor blade and a cocoon.
Following directions	2. Take the razor blade and very carefully cut through the outer layers of the cocoon.
Inferring	What does the movement tell you about the cocoon?

Teacher's Note: The larva inside the cocoon has a heartbeat. Movement indicates the larva is alive.

Measuring	3. Observe the larva and try to count the number of times the heart beats per minute.
Following directions	4. Place some cocoons in a covered jar with several air holes in the lid.
Hypothesizing	Why is air necessary for the cocoon?
Observing	5. Observe the cocoon carefully for several days. Record the number of days it takes before the changes are evident.
Collecting data	What happened to the cocoons?
Observing	6. When a moth appears, watch it closely.

Hypothesizing	What do you think will happen to it that will enable the moth to fly?

Teacher's Note: Soon after the moth comes out of the cocoon, the moth pumps blood into its wings by moving the wings up and down. The moth is then able to fly.

Observing	How have the cocoons changed in appearance?
Summarizing	What can you say about how moths grow and develop?

Part II *Polliwogs*

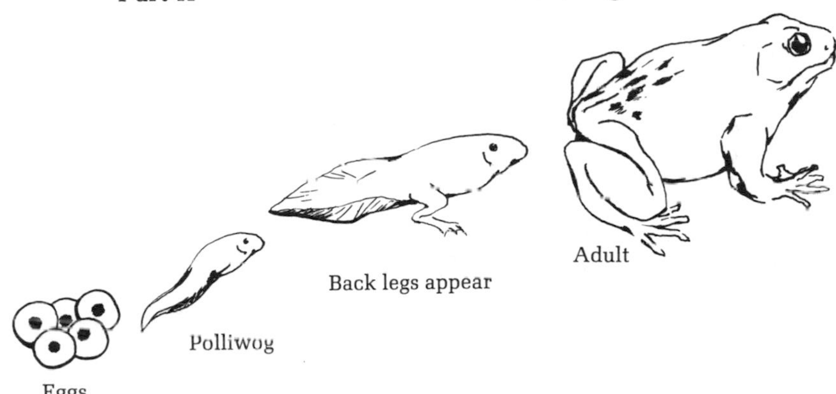

Following directions	1. Obtain some polliwogs and place them in a large jar or an aquarium containing some green aquatic plants or algae.
Observing	2. Observe the polliwogs and record any changes you see.
Summarizing	After two weeks, describe how the polliwogs have changed from the time you put them in the jar.
Comparing	How does their change compare with the way the cocoon developed?
Hypothesizing	What do you think would be the result if you did not put the green plants in the water?
Inferring	What name could be given to the changes that a frog goes through?

Teacher's Note: The frog, like the moth, goes through several changes in form during its development. This process of changing form, structure, and function in development is called *metamorphasis*.

Open-ended Questions

Hypothesizing	1. What do you think would happen to the polliwog if it were placed in very cold water and kept at a low temperature?
Designing an investigation	2. What would you do to find out if a polliwog or a snail has a heart?

Problem: WHY ARE SUCTION CUPS HARD TO PULL APART?

Grade Level: (6–8)

Concepts

A partial vacuum is a space where there is less air pressure because there is less air present in the space.

Materials

Two rubber vacuum cups (suction cups)
Spring scale
Wet sponge

Discussion Questions

(Critical thinking processes)

Inferring	What is a partial vacuum?
Designing an investigation	How can a partial vacuum be made?

Pupil Discovery Activity

(Critical thinking processes)

Teacher's Note: This activity should be done in groups of two pupils.

Following directions	1. Obtain two rubber suction cups and a sponge. Wet the sponge, moisten the

rubber suction cups around the edges with the wet sponge. Squeeze the cups together.

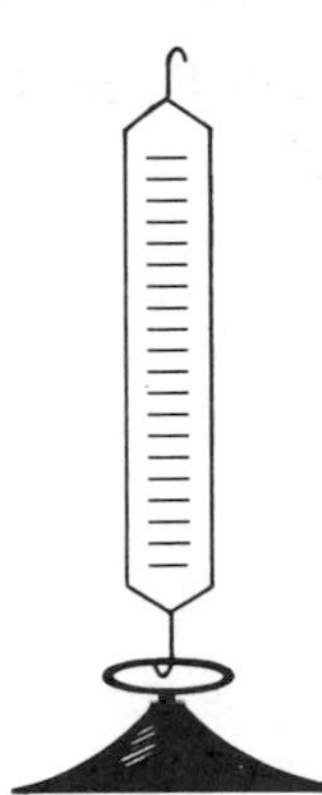

Hypothesizing	What do you think about your ability (two of you) to pull the cups apart?
Following directions	2. Try to pull the cups apart.
Hypothesizing	Why are the cups difficult to pull apart?
Following directions	3. Moisten the edge of one of the cups and push it against the blackboard.
Recording data	4. Record what happens when you push the cup against the wall.
Following directions	5. Obtain a spring scale, hook it to the cup, and pull gently. Caution: Do not pull hard on the scale and do not try to pull the cup off with it because you will break the scale.
Observing	What does the spring scale indicate when you pull it?
Hypothesizing	How much force is needed to pull the cup from the wall?

Teacher's Explanation: Find the area of the hemisphere (cup) by using the formula $2\pi r^2$, where r stands for the radius of the sphere, the distance from its edge to the center. If this is figured in square inches of area on the sphere, the total force applied to the sphere can be calculated by multiplying each square inch by 14.7 pounds of air pressure for each square inch of surface on the sphere. For example, a 10″ square level area would require about 10 × 14.7 lb/sq. in. = 147 pounds of force to pull it free under ideal conditions.

Open-ended Questions

Inferring	1. About how many pounds of air pressure per square inch is there exerted on your body?
Hypothesizing	2. On the moon there is no air pressure. What would happen to your body on it if you walked out of a rocket ship and forgot to put on your pressurized suit?
Inferring	3. Sometimes when people fly in planes, their fountain pens leak. Why does this happen?
	4. Von Guericke originally took two copper hemispheres, stuck them together, and pumped the air out of them. He then attached horses to each side of of the globes, as shown in the diagram below, and tried to get the horses to pull them apart. Less than eight teams of horses could not separate the globes.
Inferring	Why?

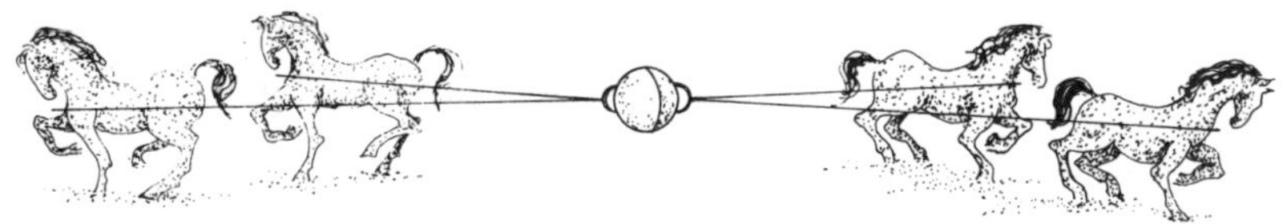

Inferring	4. What did Von Guericke do to the hemispheres so that the horses could pull them apart easily?
Hypothesize	5. If the balloon on page 139 is this size at sea level, draw about how big this balloon would be at the top of a mountain 15,000 feet high.

Directions on how to write a discovery laboratory lesson

After having looked at the preceding lessons, try to write one of your own. Follow the directions below step by step and you will design a guided discovery lesson. Once your students have become fairly skilled in following this guided approach, you should try to gradually involve them in less structured discovery activities.

Steps in Writing a Discovery Laboratory Lesson

A. This section of the lesson is mainly for the use of the teacher

1. *Problem*
   1. Decide what concept, principle or scientific process you want to teach.
   2. State the problem in the form of a question.

      Example: (This is taken from the above lesson.)

      "What Determines How Long a Candle Will Burn Under Jars?"

2. *Grade Level*
   1. The grade level should probably indicate a range in grades. This is so because there usually is a wide range in mental age and achievement levels of students in any single class. Furthermore, the kinds of mental tasks required are not specific to any grade level, but to a stage of mental development as outlined by Piaget and others.

3. *Concepts*

   List the subject matter principles and concepts you wish to teach as they relate to the problem.

Steps in Writing a Discovery Laboratory Lesson—(cont.)

4. *Materials*

Leave space for a list of materials but don't fill this section in until you have completed writing the activity section.

5. *Discussion*

1. Write questions which will set the stage of the lesson.
2. In most cases the lesson problem may be stated as one of the questions in this section. Obviously the principles and activities you will teach must be chosen before the matter can be discussed.

   For example, in the sample activity above, the following questions are asked:

   > "What happens to things when they are burned?"
   > "How do you get something to burn?"
   > "How would you find an answer to the problem?"

3. One general question you can almost always ask in this section is how they, the students, would go about solving the problem. This gives the class a chance to think of how they would design an investigation.

6. *Student Discovery Activities*

1. Decide on or consult a science sourcebook to get ideas for activities and science concepts and principles you might wish to teach.

B. The Discovery Activity part of the lesson is given to the students if they are able to read.

1. Think of ways to design the activities you selected so that the children will be called upon to do process thinking.

Steps in Writing a Discovery Laboratory Lesson—(cont.)

2. The processes that might be included are listed under "Critical Thinking Processes" below.
3. Generally the lesson is started by telling the children to collect the materials needed in the activity. This may be followed by asking them how they would use the materials to solve the problem.
4. Next ask what they think will happen if such and such procedure is done.

   Example. "How long do you think the candle will burn if you cover it with a quart jar?"
5. Ask the students then to follow the suggested procedure and observe what happens in order to test their hypotheses.

   Example: "Cover the candle with a jar and time how long the candle burns."
6. The next step would be to ask the students to record the data. Strive particularly to have them use mathematics in measuring and graphing where possible.
7. Then ask them to interpret or make inferences about the data they collected.

7. *Critical Thinking Processes*

1. Read your statements in the investigation and compare them with the following processes.

   Cognitive—Critical Thinking Processes

   Comparing
   Summarizing

Steps in Writing a Discovery Laboratory Lesson—(cont.)

Criticizing
Assuming
Imagining
Decision Making (evaluation of what to do)
Applying

Scientific Processes (Also Cognitive—Critical Thinking) but more related to carrying out scientific experimentation.)

Observing
Classifying
Inferring or Making Interpretations
Collecting and Organizing Data
Measuring
Hypothesizing or Predicting
Designing an Investigation
Operational Definition
Formulating Models
Following Directions

2. List the appropriate process by each of the questions you ask in the pupil discovery activity section.
3. Once you have done this compare your lesson with the above list of processes and see if it can be rewritten to include more of the processes. Modify the lesson to do this where appropriate. The comparing of your lessons with the process list is a way to evaluate how sophisticated your lessons are and what they require of students as far as cognitive abilities are concerned.

8. *Open-ended Questions*

Open-ended questions are questions which should suggest further possibilities for laboratory investigation. Gener-

Steps in Writing a Discovery Laboratory Lesson—(cont.)

ally, questions which might be included in this section are:

a. If you were to repeat this activity how would you improve it?
b. What other possibilities for experimentation did this activity suggest to you?

Generally, in the pupil discovery activities section, the students have tested one variable or the influence of one factor on an object or organism. They might, however, in this open-ended section, be asked questions involving the influence of other factors on the same object. This is explained in detail below.

9. *Teacher's Notes*

Teacher's Notes: Are explanations of what happen in the lesson or suggestions of how to do the lesson.

(4) *Materials*

Reread your lesson and list in the vacant space you left under the materials section those materials and equipment needed in the lesson. *Be sure to be definite in writing the quantities used in the materials section.*

For example: Don't write: "Some candles" but write "10 candles."

Be sure to check the procedure section to see that you listed accurately all the materials required.

Suggestions for Writing Open-ended Questions

In any experimental situation there are variables or factors being tested. For example, "What effect does water have on the sprouting of seeds?" What this is asking is: "What does the factor

—water—have to do with the sprouting of seeds. Look at the seed problem again. Try to write three open-ended questions which suggest further investigation.

You probably had little difficulty in doing this. All you had to do is think for a minute what might influence the sprouting of seeds. You may have thought of such factors as light, temperature, pH (acidity population), the number of seeds present, etc. Some examples of factors which may be involved in experimental conditions are listed below. You can probably think of many others. Use this list or, better yet, prepare your own to help you in writing open-ended questions.

Population density
Temperature
Light
Sound
Water or humidity
Food or presence of minerals
pH—alkalinity or acidity
Air or other gases or lack of them (space flight conditions)
Pressure
Type of motion
Fields—gravitational, magnetic, electrical
Friction
Force
Pollution

Examples of Open-ended Questions Using a List of Factors

Factor	*Example*
1. Population Density	1. What do you think would happen to the sprouting of seeds if the number of seeds were doubled, tripled, etc.?
2. Temperature	2. What do you think temperature has to do with the metal's physical characteristics?
3. Light	3. What intensity of light is needed for the plants to bloom? How would you find out?
4. Water or humidity	4. How does humidity affect the sound transmission?

Factor	*Example*
5. Pressure	5. What effect does pressure have on the growth of other organisms?
6. Friction	6. What role does friction play in the motion of the object? How could it be reduced?
7. Pollution	7. What indications are there that pollutants might have affected the results of the experiment?

TESTS

Tests are only as good as the questions they ask. What has been said in previous sections about the desirability of asking good questions has particular relevance for constructing tests. Teachers traditionally have emphasized the evaluation of knowledge. To guard against this tendency, questions can be classified according to Bloom's Taxonomy as shown below. In this way an instructor can be more certain he is teaching for the higher levels of learning. If an instructor has outlined behavioral objectives and classified them according to Bloom's Taxonomy, he naturally would not have to classify his test questions since these reflect the level of the objectives.

Level of Sophistication	*Test Questions*
Synthesis (Social Studies)	1. If you were going to improve the environment of our community, what would you do?
Comprehension (Driver Ed.)	2. Which of the following would be most helpful in bringing a car to a rapid stop? a. Tires with thick thread b. Light weight body of a car c. Magnetic wheels d. Heavy car body
Application (Science)	3. A scientist found an island far from land. No animal could fly nor swim away from it. On the island there

Level of Sophistication | *Test Questions*

were plants eaten by only one type of first order consumer. There was also a predator that ate only one type of first order consumer. The island looked as though it were biologically in balance.

——1. If all the predators were removed, which of the following would happen?

a. The other two populations would increase
b. The other two populations would decrease
c. The producers would decrease and the first order consumers would increase
d. The producers would increase and the first order consumers would decrease
e. none of the above

Three styles of evaluation

Individuals learn through three systems of representation of the world: 1. enactively, 2. iconically, and 3. symbolically. In enactive involvement an individual learns by doing something. He performs some action and may become mentally skilled as a result. He may drive a car, play tennis, make a jewel box, paint a picture, experiment, write an essay, produce a poem, run a business, etc. In iconic learning (from the Greek, an image) the individual conceptualization is based mainly on perception. He may learn by studying a picture, diagram, graph, etc. Symbolic representation[1] learning occurs by the use of written words or other symbols such as mathematical or statistical notations.

[1] For further discussion about what is meant by "representation" see Jerome S. Bruner, *Toward a Theory of Instruction* (W. W. Norton and Company, Inc., New York, 1968), pp. 11–21.

Learning Through Various Systems of Representing the World

Enactive	*Iconic*	*Symbolic*
Learns by actions 	Learns by images or pictures—perceptual based 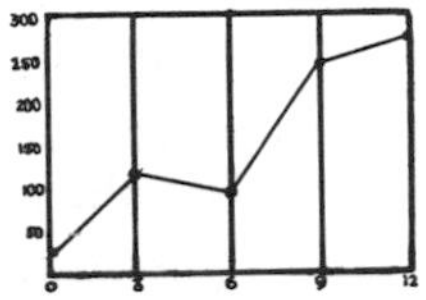	Learns by symbols 1+2=3 Cats have whiskers

Since there are these three types of learning, it seems reasonable that there should be three types of evaluation. Unfortunately, tradition-bound teachers generally emphasize symbolic evaluation. This is unfortunate because often, in using this form, the evaluator tests mainly for verbal understanding rather than subject matter comprehension. Leonard B. Finkelstein and Donald A. Hammil found in a study that many students who were evaluated mainly on written tests appeared to achieve poorly. However, when the same subject matter was evaluated using aural methods (a tape recorder) and pictures, there was no significant difference in mean scores between good reading and poor reading students. These authors are of the opinion that many tests actually evaluate reading comprehension not the conceptualization of the concepts and principles of a discipline.[2]

Teachers should, therefore, guard against the over-emphasis of reading-dependent tests. This should be obvious to most experienced teachers. It is a rare teacher who hasn't had students who clearly understand in discussions and class participation the subject matter principles, but flunk questions on paper tests. Certainly, the use of more pictorial evaluative techniques is waranted and needed. A teacher who tries to prepare such instruments soon develops his skill at devising them and gains better insights into his instructional procedures.

[2] Leonard B. Finkelstein, Donald D. Hammil, "A Reading-Free Science Test," *The Elementary School Journal* (October, 1969), pp. 34–37.

It's of interest to note that many of the new standardized tests such as the Metropolitan Achievement Tests[3] use diagrams in their testing programs.

The Pictorial Riddles given earlier in this chapter can be used as guides to how you might write iconic types of tests.

SUMMARY

Good questioning should permeate all modes of instruction. Specific techniques for applying what you have learned in this text have been outlined for using films, filmstrips, 35mm slides, film loops, and tape recorders, and for preparing taped discussions and test questions, pictorial riddles, invitations to discover, discovery bulletin boards, inquiry-oriented investigations, and tests.

The way to improve questioning techniques is to prepare questions for these various instructional approaches following the suggestions for each technique outlined in this chapter and applying what you have learned from the other chapters. To insure that you are making progress, your work should be evaluated as suggested in the next chapter.

[3] Metropolitan Achievement Tests, Harcourt, Brace and World, Inc., 1969.

8

EVALUATING YOUR QUESTIONS

Has what this book said affected your questioning behavior? Have you internalized its message? After reading the chapters, do you actually ask better questions? It is easy to read about questioning, but much more difficult to apply what is suggested. Reading this book is not enough to change your questioning ability. Old habits of questioning are hard to modify and you must consciously strive to improve your techniques over an extended period.

Your ability to lead a discussion group so that it is less teacher-centered and more student-centered probably will be difficult. For this reason you and/or other individuals should evaluate the types of questions you ask in discussions, study guides, examinations, etc., and work constantly at trying to improve them.

EVALUATING WRITTEN QUESTIONS

To insure you are becoming better at questioning, you should evaluate yourself periodically. There are three general ways to evaluate written questions:

Grouping questions as convergent or divergent

Check to see whether you have divergent questions, particularly at the first part of a discussion. If you don't, modify questions so that they are more divergent. To evaluate this type of questioning ability the following simple check sheet is suggested. You use it by marking a check in the appropriate level each time you require a response indicated. For example: If your question is a divergent one, you would mark the square below as indicated.

1. Convergent											
2. Divergent	X										

Classifying questions according to Bloom's taxonomy

Evaluate your questions by using Bloom's *Taxonomy of Educational Objectives*. Bloom and his associates have devised a classification system composed of a hierarchy of six categories. The lowest category is knowledge, and the highest is evaluation. If the

Questions	*Know-ledge*	*Compre-hension*	*Appli-cation*	*Analy-sis*	CREATIVE *Syn-thesis*	*Evalua-tion*
1. What hypotheses would you make?					X	
2. How would you solve the problem?					X	
3. What inference would you make?					X	
4. What is the name of the capitol of Rhode Island?	X					
5. What would happen to the cake if it were cooked 5 minutes longer?			X			
6. What is the most significant scene in Hamlet?				X		
7. How would you find the area of a triangle having two sides that are equal?		X				

question just requires the respondent to know something, a question should be coded as a knowledge type question. For further information on the use of the taxonomy refer to Chapter 4.

In using the taxonomy to classify questions, the chart on page 150 may be used. Questions should be written on the left-hand margin and then classified according to one of the six categories. If the questions, for example, are creative they should be classified under either the synthesis or evaluation categories. In evaluating your questions you should endeavor, as much as possible, to classify them objectively. You should not use, for example, the synthesis level unless you really think it requires a student to put together information in his mind in a form new to him.

Classifying questions for critical thinking

Evaluate your questions according to the critical thinking processes they elicit. To do this you must compare each question you have written with a list of critical thinking processes—shown below is a list of these. The list is not complete. You may as you become more sophisticated want to supplement it with additional processes you feel are unique to your instruction.

Comparing
Summarizing
Observing
Interpreting or inferring
Criticizing
Looking for assumptions
Imagining
Collecting or organizing data
Hypothesizing
Applying facts and principles
Making decisions
Designing projects or investigating
Creating
Coding
Qualifying
Quantifying
Solving a problem
Identifying a problem

Listed below are some sample questions illustrating how this classification system may be used.

Critical Thinking Analyses Inventory

Critical Thinking Process	*Questions*
Hypothesizing	1. Some fish can live out of water for a while. This is so if and only if what?

Critical Thinking Process	*Questions*
Interpreting	2. What are the main psychological conflicts found in Hamlet?
Problem Solving (Hypothesizing)	3. If you were going to improve racial relations in our community, what would you do?
Interpreting	4. From observing the automobile crash in the film, what caused it to occur?
Applying	5. You watched George pass the ball. Now what should you do when you pass the ball?
Creating	6. Given these rusty nails and wire, what kinds of things could you create from them?
Quantifying	7. How much weight is needed to balance the lever?
Identifying a Problem	8. What types of problems do you think the student government should tackle this quarter?
Applying	9. What is the most forceful way to throw a baseball?
Summarizing	10. What logical steps did you perform in solving this mathematical problem?
Creating (Hypothesizing)	11. If you were going to change this play, story, speech, recipe, directive, poem, etc., what would you do?

Please note that because some of the processes above are not mutually exclusive, you may classify them using more than one process. The important point is that you classify and evaluate your questions so that you obtain some understanding of the level of your teaching and strive to make your questions more divergent and cognitively challenging.

After you have written and classified your questions, you should spend time trying to rewrite them. The improvement of your questioning technique to implement what you have learned takes great effort and a strong desire on your part. When questioning, you should grow in your ability to the point where the discussion is mainly student-centered. Think of your role as though you were a mirror reflecting and bouncing light around the room. To bounce a discussion about a classroom while playing a minimal role takes terrific sophistication on your part; achieving this ability, however, insures greater student involvement and better learning.

THE USE OF AUDIO AND VIDEO TAPE FOR EVALUATION

Occasionally, it is wise to audio- or videotape a discussion and evaluate the types of questions you asked, i.e., how many questions were divergent, convergent? What cognitive processes were required? How much time was involved in your talking compared to student talk? If you were to lead the discussion again, how would you modify your behavior? Remember, generally the less you talk, and the more students interact, the better.

STUDENT-TEACHER INTERACTION ANALYSIS SCALES

Instruments are available to help instructors become more aware of how they spend their time in the classroom. Generally, these require some person to evaluate your class and mark on a sheet every so many seconds or minutes the type of activity taking place in the classoom. For accuracy, this person should be trained in using the analysis instruments. However, a rough approximation of the distribution of the use of time in your class can be determined by filling out the analysis inventory after the class period. If you desire a more accurate evaluation, but have no one available to make the instrument, you might audio- or videotape your class session and then play back the tape as suggested above.

If you wish to obtain a general impression of how class time is used, you might use a form such as Flander's Interaction as shown on following page.

Categories for Interaction Analysis[1]

TEACHER TALK	DIRECT INFLUENCE	1.* *ACCEPTS FEELING:* accepts and clarifies the feeling tone of the students in a non-threatening manner. Feelings may be positive or negative. Predicting or recalling feelings are included.
		2.* *PRAISES OR ENCOURAGES:* praises or encourages student action or behavior. Jokes that release tension, but not at the expense of another individual; nodding head, or saying "um hum?" or "go on" are included.
		3.* *ACCEPTS OR USES IDEAS OF STUDENTS:* clarifying, building, or developing ideas suggested by a student. As teacher brings more of his own ideas into play, shift to category five.
		4.* *ASKS QUESTIONS:* asking a question about content or procedure with the intent that a student answer.
	INDIRECT INFLUENCE	5.* *LECTURING:* giving facts or opinions about content or procedures; expressing his own ideas, asking rhetorical questions.
		6.* *GIVING DIRECTIONS:* directions, commands, or orders to which a student is expected to comply.
		7.* *CRITICIZING OR JUSTIFYING AUTHORITY:* statements intended to change student behavior from non-acceptable to acceptable pattern; bawling someone out; stating why the teacher is doing what he is doing; extreme self-reference.
	STUDENT TALK	8.* *STUDENT TALK—RESPONSE:* talk by students in response to teacher. Teacher initiates the contact or solicits student statement.
		9.* *STUDENT TALK—INITIATION:* talk by students which they initiate. If "calling on" student is only to indicate who may talk next, observer must decide whether student wanted to talk. If he did, use this category.
		10.* *SILENCE OR CONFUSION:* pauses, short periods of silence and periods of confusion in which communication cannot be understood by observer.

* There is NO scale implied by these numbers. Each number is classificatory; it designates a particular kind of communication event. To write these numbers down during observation is to enumerate, not to judge a position on a scale.

[1] Edmund J. Amidon and Ned A. Flanders, "The Role of the Teacher in the Classroom—A Manual for Understanding and Improving Teacher Classroom Behavior, p. 5." Association for Productive Thinking, Inc., 1040 Plymouth Building, Minneapolis, Minnesotta 55402. This manual suggests how to administer and analyzed the instrument.

GENERAL QUESTIONING ABILITY INVENTORY

Shown below is a general instrument for evaluating how well an instructor carries on a discussion. This sheet should be used by an impartial observer who watches a teacher lead a discussion. It may be used in two ways. The observer can checkmark one of the 21 categories whenever a teacher demonstrates one of them, or the observer makes an appropriate check every 30 seconds.

If no trained observer is available, the instructor can use this instrument to rate himself, marking it after leading a discussion. This approach is not as accurate, but can serve as an aid in suggesting to a teacher how he might improve his discussion skills. The scale also may be used in viewing video- or audiotape as suggested above.

General Questioning Ability Inventory

1. Convergent questions											
2. Divergent questions											
3. Teacher clarifies question (redefines or reinterprets)											
4. Students clarify question											
5. Discusses students answers											
6. Short teacher discussions											
7. Presents problems											
8. Calls on student for first time											
9. Students interact in discussion without teacher comment											
10. Students initiate questions											
11. Lectures											
12. Restates student statement and asks other students what they think											

General Questioning Ability Inventory

13. Reinforces students											
14. Responds negatively											
15. Accepts all responses											
16. Continues questioning even though right answer has been stated											
17. Discussion involves facts not thought											
18. Discussion involves feelings											
19. Teacher answers questions											
20. Students answers questions											
21. Teacher calls on non-volunteers											

Analysis of the questioning check list

After having placed the appropriate checks in the instrument, an instructor should spend considerable time analyzing it. A good discussion leader generally should have the following percentage of checkmarks for each of the categories:

1. Convergent questions—low
2. Divergent questions—high
3. Teacher clarifies questions—moderate
4. Students clarify question—moderate to high
5. Discusses students answers—low
6. Short teacher discussions—low to none
7. Presents problems—low
8. Calls on student for first time—high
9. Students interact in discussion without teacher comment —moderate to high
10. Students initiate questions—moderate to high

11. Lectures—low
12. Restates student statement and asks other students what they think—moderate to high
13. Reinforces students—high
14. Responds negatively—low
15. Accepts all responses—high
16. Continues questioning even though right answer has been stated—high
17. Discussion involves facts not thought—low
18. Discussion involves feelings—moderate
19. Teacher answers questions—low
20. Students answer questions—high
21. Teacher calls on non-volunteers—moderate

TOTAL TIME ANALYSIS INVENTORY

Another way to evaluate an instructor is to check the amount of time spent in each category. Videotaping is the best way to do this since the tape may be replayed to determine how much time was involved in each teaching activity. In this type of evaluation, a count in seconds is made for each procedure and the number of seconds recorded in the appropriate box. After the period of evaluation is ended, the total number of seconds per box is totaled and converted to the percentage of class time devoted to the activity. A simplified form for this procedure may be used, concentrating on those categories the teacher feels are most important. A simplified time analysis inventory is suggested for this purpose below:

Total Time Analysis Inventory

	Time in Seconds					
1. Time devoted to facts						
2. Time devoted to thought (Higher cognitive levels)						
3. Time devoted to feelings						
4. Teacher time						
5. Pupil time						

Total Time Analysis Inventory—(cont.)

Time in Seconds

6. Time devoted to redirection						
7. Teacher pauses—time for students to think						

DISCOVERY TEACHING INVENTORY

Dr. James Ashley has developed a series of questions for teachers to use in to evaluating how their teaching utilizes discovery. Since the essence of discovery teaching is to a large degree providing opportunities for student involvement and asking divergent questions, this instrument may be used to evaluate how successful you have become at providing opportunities for critical thinking and asking and responding to questions. The instrument has been modified slightly from Dr. Ashley's original form to make it more applicable for teachers at all levels. A scale has been provided. This instrument should be used as a self-evaluation inventory of the progress of your questioning ability over a semester. The inventory should be taken several times. By analyzing the results of several evaluations, you should obtain direction and suggestions for improvement.

Key Teacher Ideas[2]

A. *The Student's Experiences in the Classroom*	Seldom	Some-times	Often
1. Do you let the student decide for himself rather than give him the criterion to look for?			
2. Do you let the student generate the basis of action rather than serve as the source of knowledge?			

[2] Modified from original form the Classroom Observation Rating Form (CORF) produced by Dr. James Ashley, "A Study of the Impact of an Inservice Education Program on Teacher Behavior," unpublished Ed.D. Dissertation, University of Texas.

Key Teacher Ideas—(cont.)

	Seldom	Some-times	Often
3. Do you take time to let the student grope, ponder, or mess around rather than direct him immediately to the conclusion?			
4. Do you keep the student actively involved (either physically or mentally) rather than do the activity yourself?			
5. Do you direct students in experiences prior to expecting analysis and meaning for words rather than presenting the vocabulary before the experience?			
B. *How The Student Interprets His Experiences in the Classroom*			
1. Do you respond to explanations with questions such as "how do you know" or "is it reasonable" rather than agree or disagree with the explanation?			
2. Do you listen to student descriptions and strive for more precision rather than accept their first response?			
3. Do you help students to question explanations in terms of reasonableness of their own experience rather than accept the reasonableness of your experience?			
4. Do you recognize that one experience does not mean comprehension rather than assume because the point is clear to one, it is clear to all?			

Key Teacher Ideas—(cont.)

	Seldom	Some-times	Often
5. Do you select illustrations of an idea that are progressively less obvious than simpler ones rather than assuming that because the student saw the point in the simple illustration he sees it in all instances?			
6. Do you make students back up and simplify a complex statement so that other students comprehend rather than accept it because it sounds good?			
C. *Teacher Responses to Students*			
1. Do you keep an open mind as to the student's response rather than accept only that answer you think is correct?			
2. Do you direct student thinking by introducing situations that "don't fit" or that may be surprising rather than telling them that they don't see the point?			
3. Do you adjust the pace of the exercise to the progress of the student rather than speed to cover it or drag to fill in the time?			
4. Do you base your opinion of student performance on what you assume he can do?			
5. Do you pose questions to get students to think rather than to get the answer you think is correct?			

Key Teacher Ideas—(cont.)

	Seldom	Some-times	Often
6. Do you direct questions to the student's level rather than expect all students to operate at the same level of experience necessary to answer a question?			
7. Do you probe the basis for an inappropriate response rather than tell the student he is wrong and then search for the desired response?			

DO YOU CONTINUALLY INVOLVE THE GROUP IN THE ACTIVITY BY PROVIDING OPPORTUNITY FOR STUDENTS TO EXPRESS AN OPINION BEFORE DOING AN ACTIVITY RATHER THAN LET THE ACTIVITY BE A DEMONSTRATION MONOLOGUE BETWEEN THE TEACHER AND ONE OR TWO STUDENTS?

SUMMARY

To change your own questioning procedures takes considerable effort and time. There are several inventories to help teachers evaluate and modify their questioning techniques and insure that they improve. These instruments include: the Convergent-Divergent Analysis Inventory, classification of questions using Bloom's Taxonomy, the Critical Thinking Analysis Inventory; teacher interaction inventories such as: Flanders Categories for Interaction Analysis, General Questioning Ability Inventory, Total Time Analysis Inventory, and Ashley's Discovery Teaching Inventory, a modification of the Classroom Observation Rating Form.

These instruments may be used by trained observers of the teacher or by the instructor analyzing his own teaching through the use of audio- or videotape recordings. Good questioning technique is a very complex skill requiring superior perception, sensitivity to student needs, and creative response. It is for this reason an artistic endeavor. And, as with all artistic enterprise, there is no perfection—so too with questioning. But, just as the artist becomes fascinated with the problems of bringing excitement to a canvas, you should experience similar feelings in molding and shaping your interactions with students to bring dynamism to the learning environment. Questioning and interacting to help students become more beautiful individuals is an endeavor worthy of as much energy as it takes to to make an artistic master.

BIBLIOGRAPHY

This selected bibliography is presented to augment the practical applications of reserach on the roles of inquiry and questioning in teaching as explored in this book.

The influence of teachers' questions on both the quality and quantity of students' thinking and responses.

Aschner, M. A. "Asking Questions to Trigger Thinking," *NEA Journal* 50 (1961): 44–46.

Bellack, A. A. and J. R. Davitz. *The Language of the Classroom: Meanings and Communications in High School Teaching*, Cooperative Research Project No. 1497, Columbia University, 1963.

Davis, O. L., Jr. and Francis P. Hunkins. "Textbook Questions: What Thinking Processes Do They Foster?" *Peabody Journal of Education* 43 (March 1966): 285–92.

Gallagher, J. S. and M. J. Aschner. "A preliminary report on Analysis of Classroom Interaction," *Merrill-Palmer Quarterly of Behavior and Development* 9 (1963): 183–194.

Guilford, J. P. "The Structure of Intellect," *Psychological Bulletin* 53 (July 1956): 267–93.

Konetski, Louis C. "Instructional Effect on Questions Asked By Pre-Service Science Teachers," Ph.D. dissertation, Indiana University, 1969.

Moyer, J. R. "An Exploratory Study of Questioning in the Instructional Processes in Selected Elementary Schools," Ph.D. dissertation, Columbia University, 1965.

Pfeiffer, Isobel and O. L. Davis, Jr. "Teacher-Made Examinations: What Kind of Thinking Do They Demand?" *NASSP Bulletin* 49 (September 1965): 1–10.

Relationship between questioning and inquiry.

Bingman, Richard M. (ed.). "Inquiry objectives in the Teaching of Biology," Mid-Continent Regional Educational Laboratory and Biological Sciences Curriculum Study, Position paper 1 (2), September 1969.

Gallagher, James J. "Teacher Variation in Concept Presentation in BSCS Curriculum Program," *BSCS Newsletter* 30 (January 1967): 8–19.

Schreiber, J. E. *Teacher's Question-Asking Techniques*, Ph.D. dissertation, State University of Iowa, 1967.

Scott, N. C., Jr. "The Strategy of Inquiry and Styles of Categorization," *Journal of Research in Science Teaching* 4 (September 1966): 143–153.

Smith, B. O. and M. O. Meux. *A Study of The Logic of Teaching*, Government Research Project No. 258, University of Illinois, 1960.

Soar, R. S. "Optimum Teacher-Pupil Interaction for Pupil Growth," *Educational Leadership* 26 (1968): 275–280.

Role of reward-punishment and wait-time in questioning

Alschuler, Alfred S. *The Achievement Motivation Development Project: A Summary and Review,* Harvard Research and Development Center, Harvard Graduate School of Education, 1967 (available through Publications Office, Longfellow Hall, Appian Way, Cambridge, Mass. 02138).

Atkinson, J. W. and N. T. Feather. *A Theory of Achievement Motivation* (New York: John Wiley and Sons, 1966).

Atkinson, John W. (ed.). *Motives in Fantasy, Action and Society* (Princeton, N. J.: Van Nostrand Reinhold Company, 1958).

Goodwin, Dwight L. *Training Teachers in Reinforcement Techniques to Increase Pupil Task-Oriented Behavior: An Experimental Evaluation,* Ph.D. dissertation, Stanford University, 1966.

Kolb, David A. "Achievement Motivation Training for Under-Achieving High School Boys," *Journal of Personality and Social Psychology* (December 1965).

Kounin, Jacob S., Paul V. Gump, and James J. Ryan. "Explorations in Classroom Management," *Journal of Teacher Education* 12 (1961).

Lawlor, Francis X. "The Effects of Verbal Reward on the Behavior of Children in the Primary Grades at a Cognitive Task Typical of the New Elementary Science Curricula," *Journal of Research in Science Teaching* 7 (1970): 327–340.

Lighthall, Frederick F. and Vytautus Cernius. *Effects of Certain Rewards for Task Performance Among Lower Class Boys,* Cooperative Research Project No. S282, U. S. Office of Education, ERIC, ED 019 697, 1967 (Mimeo.).

Parton, David A. and Allen O. Ross. "Social Reinforcement of Children's Motor Behavior: A Review," *Psychological Bulletin* 64 (1965).

Rowe, Mary Budd. "Science, Silence and Sanctions," *Science and Children* 6 (March 1969): 11–13.

Sechrest, L. "Implicit Reinforcement of Response," *Journal of Educational Psychology* 54 (1963).

Questioning and affective domain

Athey, Irene. "Affective Factors in Reading." Paper presented at the International Reading Association Conference, Kansas City, Mo., April 30–May 2, 1969.

Bauer, Nancy W. "Can You Teach Values?" *Instructor* (August/September 1970): 37–38.

Kowles, David. "Research Report on the Cooperative Schools Program." Philadelphia Public Schools, 1966. (Available from Office of Affective Development, Philadelphia Public School Building, 21st and Parkway, Philadelphia, Pennsylvania.)

Krathwohl, David R., Benjamin Bloom, and Bertram B. Masia. *Taxonomy of Educational Objectives, The Classification of Educational Goals, Handbook II: Affective Domain* (New York: David McKay Co. Inc., 1956).

Lewy, Arieh. "Empirical Validity of Major Properties of a Taxonomy of Affective Educational Objectives," *Journal of Experimental Education* 36 (Spring 1968): 70–77.

Mager, Robert F. "Developing Attitude Toward Learning" (Palo Alto, California: Fearon Publishing, 1968).

Peterson, Severia. "Affective Techniques," Easlen Institute, 1254 Taylor, San Francisco, California.

Roose, Gene E. "Empirical Evaluation of Materials in the Affective Area," *Educational Technology* 9 (April 1969): 53–56.

Stevens, Warren D. "Affection and Cognition in Transaction and the Mapping of Cultural Space," *AV Communication Review* 18 (1970): 440–41.

Questioning in subject matter areas

Guzak, Frank J. "Teacher Questioning and Reading," *The Reading Teacher* 21 (December 1967): 227–34.

Rogers, Virginia M. "Varying the Cognitive Levels of Classroom Questions in Elementary Social Studies: An Analysis of the Use of Questions by Student Teachers." Ph.D. dissertation, The University of Texas at Austin, 1969.

Windley, Vivian O. "Levels of Cognition and Social Science Content in Classroom Current Affairs Periodicals." Ph.D. dissertation, University of California at Berkeley, 1966.

Analyzing teacher questioning

Adams, Thomas H. "The Development of a Method for Analysis of Questions Asked by Teachers in Classroom Discourse." Ph.D. dissertation, Rutgers, The State University, 1964.

Amidorf, Edmund J. "Interaction Analysis: Recent Developments." Paper presented at the American Educational Research Association convention, Chicago, February 1966.

Bellack, Arno A., Herbert M. Kliebard, Ronald T. Hyman, and Frank Smith. *The Language of the Classroom* (New York: Teachers College Press, Columbia University, 1966).

Carner, R. L. "Levels of Questioning," *Education* 83 (1963): 546–550.

Flanders, Ned A. *Teacher Influence, Pupil Attitudes, and Achievement.* Cooperative Research Monograph No. 12. (Washington, D.C.: U. S. Office of Education, 1965).

Floyd, William D. "An Analysis of the Oral Questioning Activity in Selected Primary Classrooms." Ph.D. dissertation, Colorado State College (now The University of Northern Colorado), 1960.

Gallagher, James J. and Mary Jane Aschner. "A Preliminary Report: Analysis of Classroom Interaction," *Merrill-Palmer Quarterly of Behavior and Development* 9 (July 1963): 183–94.

Ladd, George T. and Hans O. Andersen. "Determining the Level of Inquiry in Teachers' Questions," *Journal of Research in Science Teaching* 7 (1970): 395–400.

Harris, B. M. and K. E. McIntyre. *A Manual for Observing and Analyzing Classroom Instruction* (Austin: The University of Texas at Austin, Extension and Field Service Bureau, 1964).

Medley, Donald M., Carolyn G. Schuck, and Nancy P. Ames. *Assessing the Learning Environment in the Classroom: A Manual for Users of OScAR 5-V* (Princeton, New Jersey: Educational Testing Service, 1968).

Morse, Kevin M. "Manual for Questioning Strategies Observation System" (prelim. ed., unpublished). (Austin: Research and Development Center for Teacher Education, The University of Texas at Austin, December 1968).

Processes of discovery or inquiry as effective means of self-learning

Bruner, Jerome S. "The Act of Discovery," *Harvard Educational Review* 31 (1961): 21–32.

Carin, Arthur A. and Robert B. Sund. *Teaching Science Through Discovery* (2nd ed.) (Columbus, Ohio: Charles E. Merrill Publishing Co., 1970).

Gagné, R. M. "The Learning Requirements for Inquiry," in E. Victor and M. S. Lerner (eds.), *Readings in Science Education for the Elementary School* (New York: The Macmillan Company, 1969).

Jones, Richard M. "Fantasy and Feeling in Education" (New York: New York University Press, 1968).

Shulman, Lee S. "Psychological Controversies in the Teaching of Science and Mathematics, *The Science Teacher* 35 (September 1968): 34–39.

Shulman, Lee S. and Evan R. Keislar (eds.), *Learning By Discovery, A Critical Appraisal* (Chicago: Rand McNally and Company, 1966).

Questioning and Creativity

Cronbach, L. J. "How Can Instruction be Adapted to Individual Differences?" in R. M. Gagné (ed.), *Learning and Individual Differences* (Columbus, Ohio: Charles E. Merrill Publishing Co., 1967).

Parnes, Sideny J. *Student Workbook for Creative Problem Solving Courses* (Buffalo, N. Y.: The University Press, State University of New York, 1963).

Smith, James A. *Setting Conditions for Creative Teaching in the Elementary School* (Boston: Allyn & Bacon, Inc., 1966).

Williams, F. E. "Models for Encouraging Creativity in the Classroom," *Educational Technology* 9 (December 1969): 7–13.

Questioning and cognitive domain

Bloom, Benjamin S., (ed.). *Taxonomy of Educational Objectives; Handbook I, Cognitive Domain* (New York: David McKay Company, 1956).

Clegg, A. A., G. T. Farley, and R. J. Curran. "Training Teachers to Analyze the Cognitive Levels of Classroom Questions." Research Report No. 1, Aplied Research Training Program (Amherst: University of Massachusetts School of Education, June 1967).

Davis, O. L., Jr. and Drew C. Tinsley. "Cognitive Objectives Revealed by Classroom Questions Asked by Social Studies Student Teachers," *Peabody Journal of Education* 45 (July 1967): 21–26.

Mager, Robert F. *Preparing Instructional Objectives* (Palo Alto, Calif.: Fearon Publishers, 1962).

Neidt, Charles O., and Daiver H. Hedlund. "Longitudinal Relationships Between Cognitive and Affective Learning Outcomes," *Experimental Education* 37 (Spring 1969): 56–60.

INDEX